Continued from front flap]

Alan Jefferson here ~~~~~~~~~
life (including
recently come to
assessment of his
place in the 1970.
Song Before Sunrise
reveal how the ~~~~~~ ~~~~~~ as the best
example of Delius's tone-poems. His methods
of composition are also examined.

The book is made the more valuable by the
addition of seven appendices, which include a
list of works containing for the first time a
number of hitherto unknown compositions, a
bibliography more comprehensive than ever
before, and complete details of the three Delius
Festivals in England.

The Master Musicians Series

DELIUS

SERIES EDITED BY

SIR JACK WESTRUP,
M.A., Hon.D.Mus.(Oxon.), F.R.C.O.

VOLUMES IN THE
MASTER MUSICIANS SERIES

BACH ∽ Eva Mary and Sydney Grew
BEETHOVEN ∽ Marion M. Scott
BELLINI ∽ ∽ Leslie Orrey
BERLIOZ ∽ ∽ J. H. Elliot
BRAHMS ∽ ∽ Peter Latham
BRUCKNER AND MAHLER ∽
    ∽ H. F. Redlich
CHOPIN ∽ ∽ Arthur Hedley
DEBUSSY ∽ Edward Lockspeiser
DELIUS ∽ Alan Jefferson
DVOŘÁK ∽ ∽ Alec Robertson
ELGAR ∽ ∽ Ian Parrott
HANDEL ∽ ∽ Percy M. Young
HAYDN ∽ ∽ Rosemary Hughes
LISZT ∽ ∽ Walter Beckett
MENDELSSOHN ∽ Philip Radcliffe
MONTEVERDI ∽ ∽ Denis Arnold
MOZART ∽ ∽ Eric Blom
PURCELL ∽ Sir Jack Westrup
SCHUBERT ∽ Arthur Hutchings
SCHUMANN ∽ ∽ Joan Chissell
SIBELIUS ∽ Robert Layton
VAUGHAN WILLIAMS ∽ James Day
VERDI ∽ ∽ Dyneley Hussey
WAGNER ∽ ∽ Robert L. Jacobs

In Preparation

FRANCK ∽ ∽ Laurence Davies
GRIEG ∽ ∽ John Harton
SMETANA ∽ ∽ John Clapham
TCHAIKOVSKY ∽ Edward Garden

FREDERICK DELIUS, *c.* 1900
after a painting by Jelka Rosen Delius

THE MASTER MUSICIANS SERIES

DELIUS

by
ALAN JEFFERSON

*With eight pages of plates
and music examples in text*

LONDON
J. M. DENT AND SONS LTD

OCTAGON BOOKS · NEW YORK
1972

First published 1972
© 1972, Alan Jefferson

Made in Great Britain
at the
Aldine Press · Letchworth · Herts
for
J. M. DENT & SONS LTD
Aldine House · Bedford Street · London

Library of Congress Catalog Card Number: 77-175645

ISBN: 0 460 03131 7

PREFACE

IT HAS been said that the BBC television film about Delius secured a greater audience at its first showing than Sir Thomas Beecham managed to bring together at all his concerts in England devoted to or specializing in Delius's music. Whether or not this is strictly true is of less importance than the fact that television achieved what no person has been able to do since the death of Beecham: to gain new audiences for this most individual of any twentieth-century music.

I started to write this book long before this event and my own interest in the composer stems from the Sadler's Wells Ballet's production of a work by Frederick Ashton called *Nocturne*, based on the score of *Paris*, which I first saw in 1944. Since then my knowledge and love of Delius's music has developed until a visit to Grez-sur-Loing put the finishing touches to my conviction that a new analysis of his life and work is needed. I do not pretend that this is the most complete one, nor that the last word has been said; but I have been most fortunate in having the help and resources of Dr Lionel Carley and Robert Threlfall Esq., Archivist and Assistant Archivist respectively of the Delius Trust. They have not only read through the typescript and the proofs, but have been responsible for Appendices B and D in the book. Without their assistance and whole-hearted enthusiasm I fear that a number of important facts would have been omitted.

I have also to thank a number of others who put themselves out to help me gather information, and this I do most sincerely. They are: Mme A. Merle d'Aubigné and the late Mme L. Courmes, of Grez-sur-Loing; Basil Dean Esq. and Sir Julian Hall, of the Garrick Club, London; Ronald Moore Esq., whose annual visits to Florida helped to keep me abreast of activities at Solano Grove and at Jacksonville, and two of whose photographs are reproduced in this book with his kind permission; also Major Nigel Taylor, for having conveyed me to Grez-sur-Loing, and for having taken photographs there which are also reproduced here; and Ken Philip Esq., who copied and processed two

Preface

rare photographs. My thanks are due to Mrs Margaret Vessey and to Dora Labbette for giving me so much of their time. I am also grateful to the Courtauld Institute of Fine Arts, to the English Folk Dance and Song Society, to the French Government Touring Office, to the Meteorological Office and to the Royal National Institute for the Blind, for having answered questions; and to the Librarian and staff of the BBC Music Library for their invaluable help.

ALAN JEFFERSON

Ash, Surrey, 1965
Grez-sur-Loing, 1966
Guildford, Surrey, 1971

CONTENTS

ILLUSTRATIONS

FOR PATRICK

'It was once said of Delius that he divided English critics into two camps, those who did not know his works disputing the opinions of those who did.' Constant Lambert, *Music Ho!*

CHAPTER I

1862-84

AMONG ALL the composers who have an affinity with Britain there is one whom we call English and count as our own, although when he lived he was more a citizen of the world, claiming relationship with several countries while belonging truly to none.

Frederick Delius was born of German parents in Yorkshire. He lived all his adult life abroad and was scarcely understood in England until five years before his death in 1934. Despite his foreign parentage, domiciles and outlook, he breathes the freshness of the Yorkshire moors in his music, the peacefulness of the English countryside and a great kinship with Nature. It is a music that in its maturity is not easily related to any other; and Delius cannot be said to have founded any succeeding school of composition. He thus stands more alone and aloof than any other, and has little in common with his two main contemporaries in England: Elgar and Vaughan Williams. Between Delius and Vaughan Williams there is the interest in pastoral elements and in folksong, but Delius speaks more deeply for Nature itself.

We are concerned in this book with Delius the man, especially as emphasis on his later life has generally led to a somewhat misleading impression of what he was really like. James Gunn's famous portrait, Eric Fenby's moving book [1] and a television production first put out by the BBC in 1968 [2] all show Delius as a crippled, blind invalid, mostly devoid of humour and consideration for others; not, in fact, a very attractive person at all. Although he was exactly like this for the last eight years of his life, they are not representative of the whole. The picture they give, now all too familiar, tells us nothing of the lusty Bohemian; the witty and elegant adventurer; the *bon viveur*; the practical joker and

[1] *Delius as I knew him* (1936).
[2] *Delius* ('Omnibus' presentation), directed by Ken Russell.

I

raconteur; the man who, in his prime, was so handsome that he was greatly sought after by women. His life story is one of the strangest in musical history.

Delius's music may appear to defy analysis after casual hearing, as it may also appear to be impossible to memorize. Its elusive form and shifting harmonic structure, as well as the melodies which are often less striking than their accompanying harmonies, may well sound totally haphazard. But none of this is so. While Delius's intentions need not be entirely understood at first hearing, and often not at all from the score, they will repay concentration.

He is best remembered for his tone poems and their affinity with Nature. His direction is never towards God, nor any deity, but towards those elements and objects which God created: the seasons (especially summer), mountains, hills, water, rivers and gardens, sunset, evening, the song of birds. All these reminiscent sounds and the feeling of climate and warm air are faded in and out gently. For, as Delius reminds us all the time, nothing in Nature happens suddenly (except thunder and lightning, two phenomena which the composer ignores).

Delius was anti-religious, though essentially a good man in the sense that he was honourable, honest and obeyed most of the commandments without acknowledging their existence. It was not that he blasphemed or purposely went against the established Churches (whether in America, France or England) but that he firmly believed in the prime importance of the individual. Further, he believed that the superman is both possible and desirable, while the weak are to be despised, neither encouraged nor helped. This happens also to be the philosophy of Nietzsche, whose teachings were very much in fashion during the latter quarter of the nine-teenth century and the discovery of whose works enabled Delius to write his *Mass of Life*. The Prussians and later the Nazis were also inspired by Nietzsche, but while Delius's family and later his wife all came from Prussia he fortunately did not live to see the effects of the Nazi régime.

If the tone poems show Delius at his most successful, the operas and chamber works which he also wrote do him less justice. His own wilful nature as well as his manner of musical expression led him to evade, if not to contradict, established musical form. His concertos, in particular, are examples of this. The six operas suffer noticeably from the absence of a

SITE OF DELIUS'S HOUSE AT SOLANO GROVE
(with the fallen live oak in the background)

DELIUS'S SOLANO GROVE HOUSE TODAY
(on the campus of Jacksonville University)

strong libretto and professional construction of plot and text. As a result only four of them have ever been staged in Britain and none is what might be termed a repertory piece. This is most unfortunate because Delius was able to write for the voice in a particularly assured and successful manner. His choral harmonies, which shout 'Delius!' after a couple of bars, are not as impossible nor as ungrateful to the singers as they were at first considered to be, while the subtlety of their employment can only be marvelled at.

Delius belongs only marginally to an established school of composition and that is the loosely termed and vaguely defined 'post-impressionist romantic'. The fact that he created his own musical signature so indelibly is due entirely to his remarkable character and abilities. He had a great talent for languages; played the piano capably and the violin well; sustained the effects of appalling frustrations at the beginning of his life and again at the end; and remained aloof, remote and self-sufficient from all but a few well-chosen musical friends. As a person he was brilliant in conversation and in original thought; a connoisseur of painting; an expert in the important matters of food and wine; and a great wit.

The very way in which he chose to live and to compose may well have restricted his means of musical expression, but in so doing it did establish his individuality more firmly. The texture of his music breathes a partly indefinable quality which is unmistakable. There may seem to be less variety in half a dozen Delius works than in one movement of a Haydn symphony until one has taken the trouble to enquire into Delius's vocabulary. Over twenty-five years ago two separate and highly thought-of musicians said, respectively:

To know and love one of Delius's most characteristic works is to know and love them all.[1]

and:

... let it [his music] float past you as a dream vision of ineffable beauty ... the moment you bring reason to bear upon it the vision begins to fade.[2]

I do not agree that either of these statements holds conviction; they are

[1] Ralph Hill, chapter on Delius in *British Music of Our Time*, 1946.
[2] Edwin Evans, quoted by Ralph Hill, *ibid*.

generalizations and I believe that, despite the many changes in English, or any other, music since the 1940s (or perhaps because of these changes), Delius sounds very sane and reassuring today.

His lack of all but the barest formal teaching, his self-instruction and self-adaptation are not meant to be taken as examples to be followed by would-be professional musicians. He said of his only successful teacher, Thomas F. Ward, that he 'showed wonderful insight in helping me to find out just how much in the way of traditional technique would be useful to me. . . . And there wasn't much. A sense of flow is the main thing, and it doesn't matter how you do it as long as you master it.'

Delius mastered it. His music flows as naturally as the streams and rivers, as the winds and shafts of light that he was given to representing so graphically in sound. And if he was no Christian in the acknowledged sense, the philosophy of Nature which guided him makes a most acceptable alternative.

The end of January 1862 was not really cold in Bradford. There was no snow and only a little wind. On Tuesday, 29th January, Fritz Delius was born—their fourth child—to Julius and Elise. They lived in solid Victorian comfort in No. 1–3 Claremont,[1] a mansion of solid Victorian size for the large family which they were eventually to become.

The latest child was weak and sickly at birth and continued so for some years afterwards, as if he found the world and its inhabitants scarcely worth joining and little to his taste. He was christened Fritz Theodore Albert, all of which names he later rejected. Fritz he changed to Frederick; Theodore (meaning 'beloved of God') he put aside from the moment when he laughed during his own confirmation; and Albert (after the Prince Consort) he repudiated when he left England. He had only one urge and that was to be a musician.

The events at the time of Delius's birth are important to us as we look back more than a century to a way of life that was so vastly different from our own. Values of right and wrong, of morality and immorality, the almost divine right of parents over their children, and the infallible

[1] Delius was actually born in No. 6 Claremont, which still stands. No. 1–3 has been demolished.

wisdom of elders have all changed. Without understanding this it is not easy to appreciate how individuals' behaviour and thoughts might, in their context of time and place, be praised or condemned—or merely misunderstood. One cannot possibly judge the 1860s by the manners of the 1970s.

In January 1862 a number of giants amongst the composers were still living. The eldest in their ranks was Rossini, who was nearly seventy, composing eccentric piano pieces in Paris. Berlioz had completed *Les Troyens* in the same city; fascinated and inspired by the subject, he was nevertheless fearful of the potential difficulties of its production. Liszt was, at fifty, still at the height of his success and creative ability and in this particular year was greatly sought after all over Europe as a performer and teacher. Wagner was starting work on *Die Meistersinger*. Verdi was forty-eight and had completed *La forza del destino* for the St Petersburg Opera. Also in that city, Tchaikovsky was on the point of entering the newly formed Conservatoire of Music at the age of twenty-one, while Rimsky-Korsakov at seventeen was a naval cadet.

Delius never met any of these men nor can he be said to have profited directly from any one of them. Yet the approach to and understanding of Delius depends on knowing as much as possible about what was going on round him. Every composer tries all his life to express himself in his own way, either through a familiar medium or form or by an extension of them; or alternatively he may try to achieve new means of expression, employ new instrumentation, new dissonances, even 'new' instruments. But the force comes from inside him and so does the inspiration. While it is still there it is very personal and very solitary, until it is first heard. Then it becomes almost public property in so far as it is common knowledge and may be repeated endless times, so that we, who are given the means to understand what the composer has done, complete the cycle of creation by responding to it. Because every composer is his own island there is no reason to suppose that he is not influenced by, nor influences, his fellow creatures however much he may keep to himself—purposely or not. There is always the other consideration of how the music was made, and made to sound entirely different, by composers who lived at the same time and had suffered the same kind of training and musical environment.

Debussy, who influenced every composer from 1888 to the end of his life and from then until today, was born seven months after Delius. He influenced Delius as much as anybody else who has come under his spell. He altered the face of music by giving it a completely new dimen‑sion which, for the sake of convenience, is called impressionism. Tech‑nically what he did was to make studied use of natural overtones, employ added sevenths and ninths, and frequently suggest a vagueness and an aloofness by means of the whole‑tone scale.

Delius was an impressionist composer as well, suggesting rather than saying, implying rather than underlining. His music has also the same primeval quality as Sibelius's, but with one difference: while Sibelius is always cold and a little grim, like his native Finland, Delius manages to sound warm—warm with trees.

Delius's father was the epitome of a German. Why he emigrated from Bielefeld in the North‑Rhine Province to Bradford in the West Riding of Yorkshire is still partly unexplained. The Delius family had always served their country with distinction in an unbroken line going back to 1554, with here and there the unmistakable sign of a musician cropping up. It was in the late forties of the nineteenth century that three Delius brothers decided to emigrate one by one from Germany to England, which appeared to be a country of great promise and prosperity, par‑ticularly in the wool trade. The eldest brother, Ernst, led the exodus and made for Manchester. Julius came next and the first two were joined by Emil, the youngest brother, two years later. Ernst and Emil never married but in 1859 Julius, who had moved from Manchester to Brad‑ford, took a Bielefeld girl called Elise Krönig to be his wife. This was the age of large families and Mrs Delius provided her husband with a total of ten girls and four boys (one of each sex died in infancy), which was by no means exceptional.

Julius's word was law to his wife, children and household: he brooked no contradiction, no disobedience, nothing but complete and instant acquiescence to his orders. There was no explanation, no appeal, no change of mind or emphasis. He was a true Prussian. He had learned something about cloth in Bielefeld, which was the centre of the Prussian linen trade; he was not, however, class‑conscious in the way in which anybody in trade was considered to be beneath the professional classes in Victorian England—and below the moneyed classes even more. If any‑

thing he was caste-conscious and thus the English way of life in quiet, provincial Bradford was most distasteful to him. It was entirely at variance with what he had always believed to be the correct manner of behaviour. This is the bewildering part of his life in Yorkshire. In a later decade he would have been taken instantly for a German spy, and a theatrical one at that, yet this would have been far from the truth. He was much too unimaginative and obsessed with thoughts of making money out of the English to want to observe us more closely.

The Delius children were all brought up to speak both German and English as mother tongues and to adhere to a strictness of routine that had its effect later upon Frederick. Clare Delius, the seventh child and Fred's favourite sister, wrote a biography of him [1] in which she gives examples of their father's strictness towards them all. Not only her anecdotes but her way of describing her father give some idea of what a strange man he was: to us today, and to his own children then. Over and above these idiosyncrasies—as they appear today—Mrs Delius identified herself completely with her husband's demands. She was completely subservient to him and consequently offered no maternal bosom for her children to weep on when family conditions became intolerable. The father of the family pressed equally hard on wife and on all.

Despite many domestic hardships the Delius children all managed to maintain their equilibrium. After a weak start to his own life Fritz (as they called him) became a robust and hardy boy with athletic inclinations. He and his brothers got up to all the usual boyish tricks and, one might say, appeared outwardly to be leading a normal, healthy life. The boys might have become equally as good at football as they were at cricket were they not forbidden to play that rough and unpleasant game which their father decreed was entirely unsuitable for young gentlemen.

This picture of Julius Delius will no doubt appear to be ogrish, but there was an entirely different side to his nature which his family never saw. Julius was deeply fond of children, not especially his own either, and became one of the founders of the Bradford Children's Hospital. He treated his staff and their offspring with the greatest generosity and consideration and always took their word without question. Even when this

[1] *Frederick Delius: Memories of My Brother* (1935).

concerned travelling and business expenses he never demurred. For a man who had—in his daughter's words—'a ledger mind' this shows a curious attitude to the one element which dominated his very being in England—money. Yet neither did money come between his own children and a good education. It is known that a total of £37,000 was spent on schooling and travelling for the fourteen children, an average of more than £2,500 each. Today that might represent something in the order of £25,000 each.

From a very early age Frederick found his own liberal and gentle nature to be at odds with his father's rough and demanding one, but until there came a real need for him to test his strength he decided to keep quiet and do what he was told. Apart from running away from Bradford with his younger brother Max on one occasion, venturing into the forbidden bounds of wool warehouses, and other shows of boyish daring and high spirits, he did not find himself face to face with his father in true opposi-tion until the subject of music was raised—professional music.

He had begun to play the piano from a very early age. He played by ear and also improvised (sometimes to an audience of his parents' guests) and had developed his own natural technique that was moderately efficient, though contrary to established practice. Since Julius was fond of music in a purely amateur way and gave frequent musical evenings, the thought that one of his children was occasionally able to participate and had some slight talent was one thing; but for this child to want to become more than moderately proficient was outside his thinking. Frederick asked for a violin, boasting that when he had it in his hand he would play a tune on it straight away. He was given a violin and did so, although one can scarcely believe that he had never handled the instru-ment before. This display led to his being given violin lessons, first from a Mr Bauerkeller of the Hallé Orchestra and later from a Mr Haddock who came over especially to Bradford from Leeds.

In 1871, when he was nine, Frederick and his brother Max joined a preparatory school in Bradford, immediately opposite the family house. The journey proved time and time again to be too short, and they played truant, acting out the romantic stories which were denied them at home. Frederick's first great musical experience came to him in 1872 when he heard Chopin's E minor Waltz (Op. posth.): he was simply bowled over by it. A second sound-burst occurred when, at the age of thirteen, he was taken to Covent Garden to the first production in England of *Lohengrin*. It was sung in Italian and starred such eminent singers as Emma Albani as Elsa and Victor Maurel as Telramund. He was greatly moved by the whole performance although he had not seen one note of the music in advance. At the end of 1874 he went to Bradford Grammar School, where he failed to make any impression in normal academic work. One of his contemporaries there was John Coates, later to become a very fine English tenor. He had started his career as a baritone but later became a celebrated Siegfried and Tristan. Coates and Delius were to renew their friendship some forty years later.

Because of lack of progress at Bradford Grammar School Frederick was moved, with Max, to another establishment for some reason much favoured by Bradford parents. This was the International College, Spring Grove, Isleworth, Middlesex. The geographical situation had one instant attraction for Frederick: he was within easy reach of London and all its music. As soon as he had arrived in Isleworth he went to concerts and performances of the opera as much as possible, often in the company of a music master from the school. In the winter of 1879 Max and Frederick were prepared for their confirmation. Max got out of it by pretending to be a Unitarian (whatever he thought that might mean) but Frederick went through the service, only to be seized with a fit of the giggles at the very moment of the laying on of hands. This attitude to Christianity remained with him for the rest of his life and his attitude to religious belief in general was hardly less heathen.

When the two brothers left Isleworth it was as men, ready to enter the family business. Max, the youngest son and closest brother to Frederick, made it perfectly plain that he had the wrong temperament for the tough occupation of wool-brokering; while Frederick was told sharply that although music may be very well for leisure and pleasure it never makes money and certainly does not go with commerce. So Frederick's heyday was now over, his father said, to which he replied (to himself): 'Life is just beginning with music.'

In this year of 1881 two events had conspired to draw him into the family business. Max's decision and his temperamental nature had made him unsuitable to be brought up as a successor to his father; while

Ernst, their elder brother, had gone off sheep-farming to New Zealand. This was the first case of mutiny in the family, although, oddly enough, the connection with wool remained. Frederick was made of different stuff altogether—more calculating, more level-headed. He seemed to his parents and his sisters to be starting off in his new life with the best will in the world: anxious to learn, anxious to please, grateful for the chance of starting at the bottom of the strong and inviting ladder. His appearance and manner endeared him to everybody; he had none of his father's inhibitions about caste and was entirely at ease when chatting to the men in broad Yorkshire. This was on the surface: although he seems to have sincerely tried to get to grips with business the ever-present thoughts and desires of music were far too strong in him to be shrugged off or forgotten.

Clare Delius says in her book that one evening in his usual way Frederick returned home, rushed to the piano and started to play for dear life. Then he addressed his sisters. 'Girls,' he said, 'I loathe this business, but I'm going to give it a fair trial. If it fails, I'll definitely devote my life to music, no matter what happens, and some day I'll make the name of Delius known all over the world.' He was nineteen.

During that summer the idea was put forward to Julius that Frederick might make a good representative for the firm. His exceptional appearance and ways with people seemed to justify this proposal and Julius agreed. The young man was sent to Stroud in Gloucestershire, at that time the centre of the cloth industry in the west of England, and instantly made friends with the head of the concern, a Mr Baxter, who pressed him to put up in his own house rather than stay at an hotel. He was a great social success in Stroud and, as he found that the unused hotel allowance was burning a hole in his pocket, he quite often found himself in London, resuming his experiences of music and the opera. Julius was cheered by his son's personal successes, but in accepting them at face value made the first of what Sir Thomas Beecham called 'several perilous errors in tactics', by assuming that the boy had settled down and would continue to do so wherever he was sent. There was probably little opposition in Stroud to one of such charm and persuasiveness.

Next he was sent abroad to Chemnitz (now Karl Marxstadt), not very far from Berlin, Leipzig or Dresden by rail. These happened to be the three most flourishing musical centres in northern Europe. If Julius had tried to place his son in a more dangerous spot—so far as his interests were concerned—he could scarcely have picked on a more vital city than Chemnitz. Frederick heard his first *Meistersinger* in Berlin and in Chem-nitz found himself an established violin teacher called Hans Sitt, with whom he made great progress until the spring of 1882. 'Progress' is not a word that can be applied to the reports on Frederick which were sent back to Bradford from the Chemnitz company. A telegram ordering him to return at once could not be ignored, but his arrival in Bradford, laden with presents, was as dramatic as the life he had been leading. The presents included a dachshund for one of his sisters, the first of this breed of dog to be seen in Yorkshire. It caused an immense stir.

Once more Frederick found himself in the uncongenial surroundings of the Bradford office but now, having had a taste of freedom and of music making, the very thought of wool was even more unpalatable than before. So, banking on his achievement in Stroud, he persuaded his father to send him abroad again, this time as a travelling representative in Scandinavia. His powers as a salesman must have been considerable, for he prevailed over his father and on 1st June 1882 set sail from Hull to Göteborg and thence to Norrköping, the centre of the Scandinavian wool trade. Perhaps because Norrköping is a small and isolated place, Frederick once more achieved a spectacular success—on a personal basis —as he had already done in Stroud. But it did not last. One look at Sweden, one trip to Norway and its high and lonely places of Viking and Norse legend, and Frederick knew that there he would find the mental and spiritual freedom that had so far been denied him. Again he was recalled to Bradford with an appalling report from Norrköping, although this time he had taken the precaution of arming himself with proof of several initial, successful deals. After a considerable wrangle with his father a balance was drawn, slightly in Frederick's favour for the time being, and he was sent off again, this time to France. The centre of the wool trade there was St Étienne.

In St Étienne at the end of the last century, it appears, the only topic of conversation in any circle at all was wool. Frederick was entirely unequal to this mode of existence and even his brand of charm was useless against such devotion to trade. He was purposely being kept short of cash by his father and so decided to travel to Monte Carlo, stake all he had on the tables and sink or swim. He won sufficient to keep him in comfort, concerts and violin lessons until the inevitable telegram caught up with him and ordered him back to Bradford. On his reluctant way home via Paris he decided to call on his uncle Theodore, who lived there, and ask for his advice. The young man was becoming intolerably frustrated by his father pulling him one way and music calling him from the other. Some unbiased help was desperately needed.

He found his uncle living in great style in the Rue Cambon. He was a dandy in the style of the eighteenth century, unmarried and possessing exquisite taste. He held the traditional upper-class views about the place of the working class, yet he was a man of the world. He appreciated the arts as a connoisseur and detested commerce and those who toiled in it. Consequently he applauded Frederick's revolt against his father and all that Julius stood for, and was in a position to give the young man much comfort and assurance before he crossed the English Channel and faced his father again. Oddly enough Julius was not yet convinced that his truant son would not one day respond to the right training, for it seems that the two fits of success had somewhat blinded him to Frederick's true purpose; perhaps he was too stubborn to admit that he was in the wrong. At all events he sent Frederick off again to Scandinavia, where he most wanted to go. With his peculiar flair for languages Frederick had learned enough on his first trip to be able to speak and read Norwegian with some fluency, and he had by now cultivated the wanderlust within himself.

At this time Norway, anxious to achieve her own independence, was fostering the revolutionary spirit in free speech and free thought against the Swedes, who had absorbed Norway after the Congress of Vienna. This free thought was exactly what appealed to Frederick, and phrases in current use, such as 'the strongest man is he who stands alone', filled him with as much hope as they gave promise to the Norwegians. It was at this time that he first met Ibsen and Heiberg, dramatists in the nationalist vein and also revolutionaries in their own art. This trip was, from the Delius family's point of view, the worst that Frederick had undertaken, and its woeful results brought home to Julius the indisputable fact that his son lacked any scrap of business acumen. Yet he continued to display the most extraordinary tolerance—or optimism—and gave it out that some other member of the family might care to try his hand at taming the problem child.

Frederick was accordingly passed over to Manchester, where his uncle Ernst's recent business was in the hands of a manager. He decided to show Frederick exactly what is involved in being a manager and, using 'deep end' tactics, he placed the novice at his own desk for one day. There the young man not only realized how little he knew of the day-to-day work but was horrified at the personal problems brought to him by all levels of staff. This more than anything else made him completely aware of the fact that he must spend no more time trying to pretend that he could face the business life. It was a complete waste of time. The year was 1884 and he was twenty-two.

It so happened that fate took a hand in shaping his next move. A young man called Charles Douglas, about Frederick's age and also the unwilling son of a family business in Bradford, was anxious to leave England and sought a companion. At this time a number of adventurers from Europe were going to America, and to Florida in particular, where orange-growing was the vogue. Charles and Frederick pooled their financial resources, approached their respective parents, sought permission for extra financial backing and prepared to depart. At first Julius was enraged at the idea, for it was not his own. And in any case it was probably clear to him by this time that Frederick had no more idea of cultivating oranges in Florida than he had had of dealing in wool in Stroud, Chemnitz, Norrköping or St Étienne. But with much persistence, and by now with some insight into the best way of piercing his father's mind and his protective armour, Frederick won. He and Charles Douglas boarded the Cunard liner *Gallia* in March 1884 and sailed to Florida and freedom.

CHAPTER II

1884-94

FLORIDA, once the name of the whole of North America, is reputed to have been discovered by a Spaniard on Palm Sunday—*Pasque Florida*. The peninsula which retains this name today was occupied by the Spanish until 1763, when it was ceded to England, becoming an American possession in 1821. At the time of Delius's arrival a large number of Negroes lived there. They were first-generation freemen and freewomen, at home in a territory which until forty years before had been inhabited by Red Indians. Now that the Indians had been beaten and subdued (a form of genocide), the dark people from Africa were becoming local inhabitants instead. The River Apalachicola divides the peninsula from the mainland and debouches at the eighty-fifth degree of longitude. The river, the nearby Apalachee Bay and the Appalachian Mountains, which extend from Alabama to New York State, all reflect the old Indian name of Apalachia for America.

Delius and Charles Douglas left New York where the *Gallia* put them down and took a small boat to Florida.[1] With signed documents they arrived down the St Johns River at the Solano Grove plantation. The St Johns River joins the Atlantic Ocean east of Jacksonville and it is up this river, some twenty miles inland of the east coast on the thirtieth degree of latitude, that the site of the house and part of the former plantation are still to be found. The house itself has been moved bodily to the campus of Jacksonville University.

As soon as Delius set foot in Florida the tropical air and general surroundings went to work on him like a drug. They had not only an instant but a lasting effect on him and on his music to come. Here was the

[1] Florida is renowned for her fruit, for her costly bathing beaches and for one of the most expensive places in the world, some 120 miles to the south of Solano—Cape Kennedy.

direct opposite of the vast and silent heights of Norway. He stood
between them, absorbing inspiration from both, taking from both to
further his musical expression, which was ready to burst from his brain.
He had felt deep inside him the two extremes and he now had to place
himself at the right distance between them and begin.

Oranges were forgotten,[1] if they were ever thought of, and for the first few
days he was at Solano Delius wallowed sensuously in the sights, the
scents, the sounds and the joy of an entirely new world. The house, which
was remotely situated, had four rooms and was built on a bluff over-
looking the river. Magnolia, palm and pine trees grew all round, while
one huge oak stood nobly in front of the house, almost as a reminder of
England.

The nearest neighbours were a family called Bell, whose house was
five miles away. It was one of several elegant places, rather more imposing
than the Solano house. Mrs Bell was Norwegian and she and Delius
found much in common to talk about. Their favourite topic was Grieg
and his music. Mrs Bell acted as a sounding-board for Delius, and her
fondness for music helped him greatly at a time when there was nobody
else to lend him a sympathetic ear. His good fortune in finding such a
person close at hand was extended by another quite extraordinary event.
Douglas was taken ill with malaria and Delius went to find a doctor.
The nearest one was at Jacksonville, some twenty miles down river, but
when he arrived there the doctor was not at home. While he waited
Delius strolled round the town until he came to a music shop. He went
inside, sat down at a piano and began to play.

A passer-by, surprised at the uncommon sounds which he heard,
came into the shop to investigate, and introduced himself as Thomas F.
Ward, a professional musician and organist from New York and in
Florida for his health. Delius forgot all about the reason for his being in
Jacksonville and stayed there for several days, talking music and finding

[1] In his book *Delius* (1948) Professor Arthur Hutchings states that
'Delius always spoke of the Solano Grove as a "grapefruit farm", though
the fruit was known by the name of "shaddock" ....'. The fruit was mainly
the *citrus decumana* or shaddock (better known as pampelmousse), but there
are orange trees as well, as a recent visitor to Solano has testified. The pampelmousse is a cross between a grapefruit and a pumpkin.

in Ward the ideal companion and teacher. He brought his powers of persuasion into effect and managed to get Ward to move to Solano on an indefinite basis. Meanwhile, on the plantation, a neighbour had called and had taken care of Douglas, who decided that he had better move too, nearer to people who responded more actively to errands of mercy.

The new ménage at Solano Grove was a great success. A piano soon arrived from Jacksonville and for almost six months Ward instructed his avid pupil in the art of strict counterpoint and fugue, which he absorbed with all the will in the world—often working half way through the night as well as all day; lessons in orchestration were based on Berlioz's treatise. Ward was a natural and gifted teacher. Had his own musical knowledge or his teaching ability been lacking, the effect on Delius's subsequent career might have been disastrous; but this was not the case. Delius said many years later that only Ward had taught him anything worth while. Ward was the illegitimate son of a Spanish priest and was an ardent Catholic (he had been brought up by the Jesuits). Although he certainly raised the subject of religion—especially Christianity—with Delius, his interest met a complete blank.

Occasionally the two of them took a trip to Jacksonville for organ lessons at the Catholic church. More often, however, their walks and expeditions were in the nature of alligator and quail hunts, accompanied by their Negro servants, and these were just as instructive. Delius liked to listen to these innately musical people singing their old slave songs in harmonies that were far too beautiful to have been influenced by mis-sionaries. Joy in and ability to make music was so deep in the Solano Negroes that for the rest of his life Delius liked to be reminded of their songs—the old songs which had their roots in Africa and their formation in America. (There was one man who had the unusual ability to whistle in thirds.) This folk music was passed on by ear and by memory and Delius made good use of it.

In July a representative from the Delius business arrived at the grove with the intention of taking up an option to buy the whole estate. This was put into effect in August and now that Douglas had no further appetite for Solano it all became the property of Julius Delius. This incident may be explained if Ward—as is conjectured—wrote to Julius about his son, told him of their meetings and his own presence at Solano and emphasized Frederick's powers of persuasion and his industry and ambitions. He may even have suggested a music course at Leipzig, but if this was indeed the case the answer was a firm 'No'. So the move to strengthen Julius's own position by making Frederick as dependent upon him and the firm as he had been in England came about. The Delius representative sent from Bradford was called Tattersfield. Apart from the fact that he was not properly dressed for the climate of Solano, he was greatly ill at ease there. This Frederick did little or nothing to alleviate. Music, not fruit, was the entire influence and occupation of the inhabitants of Solano Grove; being entirely unmusical, Mr Tattersfield soon returned, bewildered, to make his report to Julius in Bradford.

Two months later, in September 1884, Thomas Ward returned to Jacksonville to take up the post of organist at the Catholic church, leaving Delius alone with his servants to enjoy the kind of freedom which he had never so far experienced. It was now that he began to find himself. He had started to compose, and a polka for piano called *Zum Carnival* was published a few months later in Jacksonville, not without some assistance from Ward, one suspects. Delius knew that he must go to the only place where his musical education might rapidly be furthered and that was to Leipzig. But since he was the sole custodian of Solano he could not leave it and break his promise to his father. Once again the remarkable intervention of a third person changed the situation.

After several months of hearing only Negro voices Delius was amazed one day in November 1884 to hear a European voice singing in English. The new arrival was none other than his brother Ernst. He had been sheep-farming in New Zealand for the past four years but cared neither for the New Zealanders nor their sheep. He had crossed the Pacific with nothing but a jar of whisky and his brother's address and arrived with the whisky all finished, his pockets empty, and in need of a loan. Instead of getting hard cash Ernst was persuaded by his brother that orange-raising was just the thing for him. Frederick was instantly able to absolve his conscience of the promise made to his father to stay there; he eased Ernst very rapidly into the fruit business and prepared to leave America. He stayed until after his twenty-third birthday in January 1885, when he left Ernst in sole charge of Solano Grove and departed for Jacksonville.

He taught music and also sang in the local synagogue, where his name alone allowed him to pass as a member of the Jewish faith.

An advertisement in the Jacksonville newspaper for a professor of music attracted Delius's attention and he applied for the post, enclosing glowing testimonials from both Ward and the rabbi of the synagogue. The place was Danville, Virginia, more than 500 miles to the north of Jacksonville, and the job was to teach music to the daughters of one Professor Ruckert, with only board and lodging provided. The publicity he would receive was considered an added incentive, for parents in Danville were likely to ask the new professor to give private lessons to their own children. He arrived in Danville with nothing but a dollar in his pocket and his fiddle under one arm. Widely advertised as the 'cele-brated Professor Delius', he at once settled down and his charm and elegance of manner made him a social lion. To show his proficiency on the violin he played the solo part in a performance of Mendelssohn's Violin Concerto at the Roanoke Female College in Danville. This brought him many private pupils from the families of the tobacco planters, friendships with the men and a good deal more than mere admiration from the mothers and daughters. He also gave lessons in musical theory, in German and in French.

While the actual job he was doing cannot have soothed Delius's rest-less spirit it at least gave him financial independence for the first time. He was resolved to go to Leipzig as soon as he had accumulated sufficient funds to be able to pay for the fare to Germany and his subsistence for one year. Several friends he made in Danville, aware of this struggle with his father's avowed and insistent views on the matter, were anxious to help. One of these, a Mr Phifer, wrote to Julius, praising Frederick's accomplishments and musical talent and stressing the importance to him of a professional training. But again these pleas fell on deaf ears, especially as Julius had not heard directly from his son since he left Solano.

In the spring of 1886 Delius departed from Danville, leaving (it is said) a number of broken hearts behind him. He went to New York, where his exact movements are unknown: he seems purposely to have disappeared. He spent a short time with a Jacksonville friend on Long Island and is thought to have been engaged as a church organist in Manhattan. What-ever he did proved yet again that he was able to scratch along and make a living out of music, and this fact did not escape the attention of a private detective, sent by Julius, who eventually ran Frederick to earth and delivered a message from Bradford. This said that if he went home his father would tell him that an eighteen-month course at the Leipzig Conservatorium was agreed, but with one proviso. After completing it he must return to America, where with suitable teaching qualifications he would no doubt be in a position to support himself completely.

This volte-face on Julius's part can be explained easily enough. He had installed his son in a safe job on two occasions: first in the wool trade, then in the fruit business. Frederick had left both but had still managed to keep himself going by one method or another. He had also—entirely on his own initiative—made friends and through the medium of music had been a complete, though small, success among strangers in a foreign land. He had pluck, and perhaps the course he was after might give him the status of teacher, with certificates to prove it. Julius wrote to Mr Phifer, received further corroboration and approval of his plan and then had Frederick found and brought back. But the proviso was there. After the Leipzig course (for which Julius paid) Frederick must return to America, which was, as Julius had always stressed, the land of promise. Meanwhile Ernst, true to form, had left Solano and had disappeared again. He was later heard of in Sumatra and then returned to New Zealand, where he died without seeing any of his family again.

At the end of June 1886 Delius sailed for England on the *Aurania*. After only a few days in Bradford he made straight for Leipzig, where he enrolled at the Conservatorium in August. There was no touching, biblical scene between father and son, no reconciliation. They still thought in their own ways: Frederick had got his desire against the stiffest opposition and hazards; Julius was in fact giving in—temporarily. And so for the time being they were both content.

There is no comparison today between any city in the world and the Leipzig of 1886. No contemporary centre of music comes anywhere near the power and the glory of Leipzig as it was then. There were five musical enterprises that together made it such an important place, although one of them alone was enough to be wondered at. These inbuilt institutions were the Choir School of St Thomas, the Gewandhaus and its concerts, the publishing house of Breitkopf and Härtel, its organ the *Allgemeine*

Musikalische Zeitung and the Conservatorium itself. The oldest of these was the Choir School, which served each of four churches in the city and whose sixty boys sang together once a week under the Cantor.[1] The Gewandhaus concerts originated in the eighteenth century and soon became internationally famous not only for their inherently high stan' dards but also on account of the celebrities who came to conduct them. *Gewandhaus* means literally 'cloth hall'—an unexpected reminder to Delius of the family business. While he was there Brahms, Tchaikovsky and Wagner all conducted their own works in either the Gewandhaus or the Leipzig Opera. The *Allgemeine Musikalische Zeitung*, founded in 1798, had circulation throughout Germany and was a most powerful paper.

The most recent enterprise was the Conservatorium, inspired and founded by Mendelssohn, who was also its first director when it opened in 1843. Two of the early students, Karl Reinecke and Salomon Jadassohn, were professors in Delius's time there; Reinecke had been a founder student in 1843, then already a prodigy. He was still a marvellous professor of piano. Hans Sitt was an equally capable violin teacher but the remainder, including Jadassohn, were either past their best years or else were ineffectual. Delius condemned the majority of the teaching staff and their lectures and after the first few months he tended to stay away from organized instruction. There was plenty of music apart from them, such as discussions with intelligent fellow students like Percy Pitt, who later became prominent at Covent Garden as Richter's protégé and after that at the BBC. Robin Legge, who was to be most helpful to Delius as music critic of the *Daily Telegraph*, lived in Leipzig but was not a student at the Conservatorium.

The Leipzig opera was considered in 1886 to be better than those of Dresden, Munich or Vienna. Artur Nikisch came to conduct *Tristan*, while Angelo Neumann and Gustav Mahler were to be seen regularly on the rostrum. At the Gewandhaus Brahms had conducted his Fourth Symphony as early as 1885 and came twice a year, while Tchaikovsky also came regularly to give concerts of his own works. The famous Brodsky Quartet performed the whole of the last Quartets of Beethoven, played in an exemplary fashion. Delius was glad to be able to renew his

[1] Between 1723 and 1750 the Cantor had been J. S. Bach.

FRONT OF THE HOUSE AT GREZ TODAY

GAUGUIN'S *NEVERMORE*

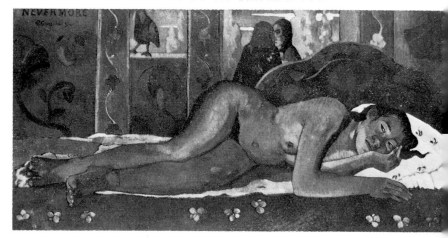

friendship and lessons with Hans Sitt, the violin professor of his Chemnitz days.

Soon after he had arrived in Leipzig and settled down he attended a performance, given by the Brodsky Quartet in the Kammermusik-Saal, of Busoni's new quartet. He met the young composer afterwards. Tchaikovsky was also present but criticized the work for its 'classicality'.

The first term passed quickly enough for Delius, and in the New Year of 1887 he found himself more and more in the company of Norwegian students with whom he was able to brush up his knowledge of the language. Conversation in several languages not only served to sharpen his wits in argument and in practical jokes, but also gave all the students a quick facility in transposition exercises, which were part of the curriculum. In the summer recess Delius and several Norwegian friends went to Norway on a walking tour. While he was there, his friends introduced him not only to Christian Sinding but also to Grieg. Perhaps because Delius was a little older than his contemporaries, and certainly far more mature in outlook, he very soon became on the friendliest of terms with these two Norwegian composers. Grieg was then forty-four and the acknowledged national composer. Sinding was thirty-one and although little known abroad had an imposing list of compositions to his credit.

Grieg gave a party to which Delius, Sinding and Johan Halvorsen were invited. Halvorsen was also a composer and a virtuoso violinist. He was twenty-three at the time; later he married Grieg's daughter. There were two ingredients at this party—schnapps and a new composition by each one of them which would be played and criticized. Delius's offering was the *Sleigh Ride*, but the quantity of schnapps which was drunk prevented this or any music from being played that night. The return to his beloved high hills, especially after Florida, inspired Delius to get down to composition in earnest. It is clear that he modelled his style on Grieg's at this time, for which he was duly criticized, but composition cannot have come easily to him when he had no idea what he would be doing in another few months' time.

The first of his works to be performed was the *Florida Suite*, for full orchestra. This was rooted in Solano and completed and scored during the two years that followed. The work has been published as an op. posth. in the collected edition started by Sir Thomas Beecham.

After a very quiet, shimmering start an oboe theme comes through the orchestral texture, reminiscent at first sight of Smetana's *Ma Vlast*. This leads into a full exposition of *La Calinda*, later to be associated with the opera *Koanga*; this version, however, is far less taut than the operatic one. The second movement of the suite has a haunting theme which tends to become tedious with repetition. The third movement contains an undoubted version of 'I've got plenty of nuttin''—to give it the name it has in Gershwin's *Porgy and Bess*—followed by a dance of Spanish flavour which probably originated with the Spanish settlers in Florida, who passed it on to their descendants and who in turn gave it to the Negroes and thus to Delius. He brought it back again to Europe. In the last movement the second theme is very reminiscent of Grieg and this whole movement is the least Delian and the least effective.

The usual way of getting student works performed in Leipzig was by engaging the musicians of Herr Bonorand's restaurant in the Rosenthal Park on the edge of the city. With a hundred marks to the leader and free beer for the players young composers were able to take heart or become depressed by what they heard. Hans Sitt rehearsed and conducted Delius's work and it was played to an audience of two: the composer and Grieg, who happened to be in Leipzig. It is a pity that his comments have not been preserved. Some songs, part-songs for mixed voices and a tone poem called *Hiawatha* also belong to the Leipzig period.

Delius's last term was due to end at Easter 1888. The unwilling promise which his father had drawn from him began to weigh oppressively, for to return to America—any part of America—was inconceivable after Leipzig. He sent a number of his compositions to Grieg and asked for his unbiased opinion in the hope that he might use anything of value as ammunition. Grieg's reply was courteous and satisfying in that he recommended a continuation of study in whatever surroundings suited his genius best. The purposeful use of the word 'genius' by an established composer is noteworthy and from what we know of Grieg it came from the heart.

The course ended after about twenty months and Delius returned to Bradford at the end of March. He heard that Grieg was going to make his début in London as pianist and conductor in early May at St James's Hall. He made two or three alternative suggestions about meeting

Grieg and his wife but they were at first received with less than the customary warmth. It turned out that Grieg was unwell and did not recover until he reached John Augener's house on Clapham Common, where he and his wife were staying while in London. Another letter from Delius was waiting for him there, inviting the Griegs to dine on the evening after the conert. Naturally Delius attended this concert, on 3rd May, at which Grieg played his own Piano Concerto and conducted his two *Elegiac Melodies*. The remainder of the programme consisted of the English première of Bizet's suite *Jeux d'enfants* and two of Grieg's songs, sung by Carlotta Elliot and accompanied by the composer at the piano. The Philharmonic Orchestra was conducted by Frederick Cowen in the concerto and in the Bizet piece.

On the following evening the Griegs met Delius at the Hotel Metropole in Northumberland Avenue and the young man put his plan to them. This resulted in Grieg writing to Julius Delius in Bradford, inviting him to dinner in London in order to discuss 'a matter of the utmost urgency'.[1] Julius was highly flattered and accepted with some excitement.While he heartily opposed music as a career for any of his children, he was very fond of it himself and was by no means untutored as a responsive listener. To meet Grieg face to face and to sit with him at table would give him immense prestige in Bradford when he returned there to recount the events of his evening in London.

The 'matter of the utmost urgency', Julius undoubtedly guessed, concerned Frederick; and when it was put to him by Grieg he was ultimately convinced that he had an exceptional son. He agreed to call off the threat of a return to America and bowed to the wisdom of Norway's leading composer. Frederick had played his cards well. Again he was saved, and Julius agreed to continue his allowance of £104

---

[1] I cannot help feeling that since this letter from Grieg to Julius was inspired by Frederick, the former one in the shape of a testimonial was likewise the result of collusion. Sir Thomas Beecham puts the reason for the letter's formality as a lack of familiarity between Grieg and Frederick. In the light of their meetings in Leipzig and Norway and especially at the schnapps party, as well as the tone of Grieg's subsequent letters, I do not consider this possible; Grieg's influence and assistance in Frederick's career must not be so lightly disposed of.

a year without any increase. This did not unduly dismay Frederick because he had already been making overtures to his uncle Theodore in Paris. He then went to stay with him in the Rue Cambon during the summer of 1888. From then on Theodore was to exercise a profound influence, even to stand *in loco parentis* to his nephew. Living in Paris can still put a fine edge of civilization onto a person's character and manners, and after many years there Theodore was a very civilized person indeed. These were the late 1880s. Delius certainly copied his uncle, and forty years later he was still behaving in this outmoded manner.

The Paris of 1888 has been captured and held for ever by the Impressionist painters: Degas, Manet, Monet, Renoir and Pissarro. Then Gauguin shattered their carefully conceived ideals by something more brutal but, in truth, more lifelike. Delius was about to be plunged into the middle of this artistic *mêlée*.

After a trip to Brittany, where he explored the wildest scenery that France can offer, he returned for a brief holiday to Norway, where he made a short walking tour with Grieg and Sinding. He then went back to France and settled outside Paris in Ville d'Avray, on the road to Versailles. It was peaceful and inspiring there and led him into an entirely new phase of life.

He began to turn his thoughts towards the composition of an opera, with the plot based on a fairy tale. This was *Irmelin*. He chose to imitate Wagner and to write the libretto himself but regrettably he possessed nothing of Wagner's dramatic instinct. The opera is almost strangled by poor construction, a lack of characterization and character development, badly placed climaxes and an absence of interest. Delius set great store by *Irmelin* and received the approval of both Grieg and Messager on this large-scale work. Their approval was almost undoubtedly on the musical side alone, but since an opera must also have dramatic and visual interest it is possible that Grieg in particular, not an opera composer himself, overlooked the other aspects and concentrated his criticism on the score alone. Florent Schmitt, a pupil of Fauré and Massenet and a most skilful orchestrator, later made the piano score of *Irmelin*; but the opera did not reach the stage until 1953, almost twenty years after Delius's death.

Delius was living just outside Paris but spent some time in the city, meeting friends there for meals and conversation. He left Ville d'Avray in

October 1889, having been there for about a year, and moved to the village of Croissy. In the summer of 1891 he took the lease of an apartment in the Rue Ducoüédic, No. 33, on the edge of Montparnasse. Throughout this time he frequently visited an artists' restaurant in the Latin Quarter. Its owner was a Madame Charlotte Caron and it was known as 'Mère Charlotte's'. The *crémerie*—to give it the French name—was run as a kind of hostel in the Rue de la Grande Chaumière, a street of students that still exists.[1] But it was a hostel with a difference. Mère Charlotte mothered all the young men, sometimes lent them money and always gave them extensive credit providing that they left a picture or carving by way of security. Among the students of nearly every European nationality, as well as an American or two, speaking their own languages, all jumbled up with Alsatian-French learned from Mère Charlotte, were the artist Alphonse Mucha, founder of Art Nouveau, the painter Sérusier, Slewinski (a Pole), as well as others who were never heard of again, the strange, tortured dramatist Strindberg and Frederick Delius.

The inhabitants of the *crémerie* were constantly changing but the place remained exactly the same, as all such institutions tended to. It is accurately described by Strindberg in the stage directions to his play *There are Crimes and Crimes*, which is set there. At the entrance were 'two resplendent boards for the greater glory of the establishment, the one with a floral theme painted by Slewinski and the other of fruit by Mucha'.[2]

Delius was on specially close terms with Strindberg, who was already showing signs of insanity. They had a common interest in the ideology and writings of Nietzsche; and, perhaps as a result of this strange harmony of discordant thought, Delius used (lightheartedly) to help Strindberg with weird experiments in alchemy and the occult. The craze for the occult was spreading throughout the inhabitants of the *crémerie* and, although Delius was above the average age of students there, no one in that close community was able to resist the current vogue.

The stuffy place was a breeding-ground for the modern style. Each would bring in some new experience, pass it on to others and thus impulses were

---

[1] It is to be found running north-east from the Vavin Métro, but all traces of the *crémerie*, No. 13, have vanished.
[2] Jiři Mucha, *Alphonse Mucha: His Life and Art* (1966).

spread, like ripples on a lake. Through Durrio, for instance (a Spaniard who cut jewellery) they carried as far as the new group forming at Montmartre . . . and became one of Picasso's first points of contact when he arrived in Paris [in 1904]. Durrio let Picasso have his studio at the Bateau Lavoir and gave practically all his earnings in support of the 'Picasso Band'.[1]

There is no word about there being another musician at the *crémerie*. The other Englishmen were artists 'adding to the fervour for the teachings of William Morris'. Delius was very much at home among these young artists and writers and their company drew him back from time to time when he had ceased to live in the French metropolis. There is no doubt that the freshness and stimulation of eager young minds at Mère Char-lotte's filled a necessary gap in Delius's education—the student life which he had never previously shared.

At the beginning of 1891 Gauguin made his appearance in Paris and at the *crémerie*. He was introduced to the company by Mère Charlotte as 'a sailor who is also a painter'. He was an excellent story-teller and had the ability to hold an audience completely under his spell while he was talking. He expounded theories on Art and Nature which he had taken from others and moulded to his own use, and had much to tell about the beauties of the tropical islands which he had already visited. As an artist he had no peer at the *crémerie*, even then, but he was difficult as a man: he was noisy and quarrelsome and drank too much. When he left Mère Charlotte's for the last time in 1895 and went to Tahiti he gave her a number of carved objects, including a saucer and five wooden engrav-ings as well as a painting (unidentified) of two Tahitian women.

The good fortune which followed Delius everywhere did nothing happier than planting him in this milieu. It certainly broadened his out-look and experience, while the conflicting views and talents of Strindberg and Gauguin added new dimensions to his own ideas. The close association which he had with the great artists of the time evoked a good deal of respect from Sir Osbert Sitwell, who said some fifty years later: 'He was the one Englishman I have ever met who knew personally the giants of the post-Impressionist Movement, recognized them for what they were and was privileged to frequent their studios. He used for example

[1] Jiří Mucha, *op cit*.

regularly to attend the Sunday evening at-homes of the Douanier Rousseau, social occasions that now . . . exhale a legendary quality un-rivalled in the art history of a period comparatively near to us. Thus Delius linked the present day to a fabulous past. . . .' [1]

In the artistic Paris that was open to him Delius inclined more to the society of artists and writers than to that of musicians. Anatole France, Guy de Maupassant, Paul Verlaine (for whom he had great admiration) and Émile Zola were acquaintances of his, but he had no association with Fauré, Gounod, Massenet or Debussy. Debussy was a few months his junior yet was destined to have more lasting effect upon twentieth-century music than any other composer of the time. 'Palely lascivious' was Delius's description of Debussy's music; with Bizet's he seemed to have a love-hate relationship, at one time deriding his work and the next moment praising it. His violin exercises at Solano Grove had nearly always been passages from *Carmen*.

Delius greatly enjoyed every side of Paris which was presented to him, and sought to discover others which were less obvious, even less attractive. There is much in any great city—and in Paris particularly—to entertain the more curious explorer, and Delius did not shun the low life. Some-times he went to look at human remains in La Morgue; the very sights and sounds and smells which had been forbidden him in Bradford were there in Paris to be experienced to the full. He spent the summer of 1891 in Norway again, and returned in a more sober frame of mind to Paris and to work in the early autumn. He had, it seemed, had his fill of mere frivolity and the underside of the city and was now seen more often in the Parisian drawing-rooms and at the soirées of fashionable society. All the same he did not entirely neglect his true friends on the Left Bank.

The musical world all round him which Delius professed not to notice must not escape our reference. Maurice Ravel and Florent Schmitt, both junior to Delius in age, shared a little of his confidence and friendship; and while André Messager, whom Delius first met at his uncle's house, was not exactly a close friend he had great respect for Delius's work and never neglected to tell him so. Of the composers named as being alive and working at the time of Delius's birth, the old order of Wagner, Liszt and

[1] *Great Morning* (1948).

Berlioz, had passed. Tchaikovsky died in 1893, Brahms in 1897; but Verdi, Wolf and Mahler all lived until the turn of the twentieth century. The new generation of composers which was emerging included Debussy and Ravel in France; Stravinsky in Russia; Richard Strauss and Mahler in Germany and Austria; and Elgar and Vaughan Williams in England. Delius had not yet emerged at all. His was a very slow start indeed. But instead of becoming bitter or frustrated at his non-acceptance he put all his energies into composition and the gradual fruition of his own style, stocking his shelves with finished works in the confidence that they would one day be heard.

Irmelin was his first major composition. The libretto was written and composition started at Croissy in 1890 and it was finished in the Rue Ducoüédic in 1892. The story tells of a princess called Irmelin who persists in rejecting suitors and of a Parsifal-like young minstrel (really a prince) of the utmost purity and naïveté. His altruistic quest for a silver stream is interrupted when he is captured by brigands but he escapes during a modest kind of orgy and finds his stream and the Princess Irmelin as well. It is a simple plot set in mediaeval times; neither the characters nor their motives demand any interest from the spectator. The words are uninspiring and at times verge dangerously upon the comical. It is not surprising that it took so long for the opera to be produced and then for only five performances.[1]

Despite these criticisms Delius did not fail with the score. The amount of thematic material that he employs is small and, while he tends to be repetitive, there are sections of the three acts which he invests with real musical interest. His golden thread of sound is kept going—the 'flow', as he called it, like the stream in the back of the hero's mind—and in its pastoral moments the work is telling. But despite his carousals at the *crémerie* Delius seemed unable to write convincingly for the brigands or for rough people of any sort. This lack of conviction is noticeable throughout the characters in *Irmelin*, particularly in the first act. From then on one is

[1] These were at the New Theatre, Oxford, in May 1953, four of them under the dedicated baton of Sir Thomas Beecham, whose idea the whole production was. It may have been that Delius never expected *Irmelin* to be staged, for as time went on and it lay on the shelf he made use of a small part of it in a separate context. See page 88.

more able to enter into this fairy-tale kind of atmosphere. The opera opens with a duologue between the Princess Irmelin and her maid, but with hidden voices calling to Irmelin about a secret lover. The maid at one point says to her: 'Child, thou art mad, such talk becomes thee ill.' When the King (Irmelin's father) brings three prospective husbands into her room in the castle, they are only knights, not princes. It is a casual kind of story, full of inconsistencies and historical errors and all bound up in a child's picture-story kind of English:

> Maid: Why look for lovers in the air
>   Thou'lt surely never find them there!
>   Thou art always looking in the sky
>   When many noble knights are nigh.
> Irmelin: Knights for thee but not for me.
> Maid: Why not for thee and why for me?

Simultaneously in the forest the hero Nils is aware of somebody waiting for him; and it is here, in the second act, that the story begins to glow, when he obtains leave from his master to search for a silver stream. This leads him to Irmelin and he arrives in time to make her leave a knight to whom she is to be unwillingly married and go away with him, after a pause in the action of this third act has allowed them both to change their clothes. At the end of the opera there is the most surprising stage direction of all: '*Irmelin and Nils wander hand in hand joyfully through the wood wondering at and discovering new beauties everywhere. The castle disappears . . . Irmelin and Nils now disappear from sight.*' Are we to take it as a complete fantasy? One does not know. In the only production of the opera that there has ever been the crude scenery mitigated any such possibility; however, the work may perhaps achieve more of what Delius intended if listened to in a broadcast form—it has been broadcast twice.

While working on a large canvas an artist sometimes seeks relief by doing another job on a smaller scale. Delius worked like this, and while the major task of *Irmelin* was in progress he started *Légendes* for piano and orchestra; but it was never completed. He also wrote three songs to words by Shelley, in which he captured to perfection the ardent approach of a young lover. These are *Indian Love Song, Love's Philosophy* and *To the Queen of my Heart*. It is interesting to find that even though these songs were written at a time overlapping the very Delian texture of *Irmelin* they themselves are not truly Delian in atmosphere. The second and third songs in particular use moderately conventional harmonies and pro-gressions; yet they all show that the composer had mastered the art of song-writing. He knew very well that the musician's function is not to embellish the words with original ideas but rather to extend the poet's mood and words within the same ambience by clothing them in music.

The song *Love's Philosophy* appears at first to be an uneventful setting, with the words over a *vivace* running accompaniment of arpeggios in the left hand while the right hand marks out a crotchet-minim-crotchet rhythm. At the end of the first stanza, when the pace slows, we get a hint of what is to happen at the end; but when it comes it is very exciting and, at first hearing, something of a shock. The running bass stops and a real Delian progression gives the composer away at once.

A song cycle followed these three Shelley songs, based on Tennyson's *Maud*. It is surprising to find Delius selecting such Victorian and English sentimentality for setting. The five songs end with *Come into the Garden, Maud*. They are unpublished and there is at present no way of contrasting Delius's and Balfe's settings [1] even if such an exercise were in any way a productive consideration, for it is Balfe's melody which will always be conjured up by the five words of the title.

By 1892 Delius composed a work called *Sur les cimes* (On the Heights, or *Paa Vidderne*), from a poem by Ibsen, and labelled it 'Tone Poem'. This musical form, which allowed the utmost freedom, had first been developed by Liszt. It reached complete and poetic fulfilment in the twenty or so tone poems which Delius wrote, irrespective of whether he labelled them variations, nocturne, fantasy, rhapsody and so on, and whether or not he used voices. Strauss's *Don Juan*, dating from 1888, was already familiar to Delius, who never ceased to be thrilled by it and heard it whenever he was able. Strauss's four other tone poems between *Macbeth* in 1888 and *Ein Heldenleben* in 1898 show how two composers' thoughts can diverge. Delius never finished expressing himself through

[1] Arthur Somervell was another English composer who set these Tennyson songs—probably with an eye, in each case, to popular taste. It is somewhat odd to find Delius in Paris with Tennyson at his elbow when he had Verlaine round the corner.

the medium, whereas Strauss found that he had said his say in it before the turn of the century.

Sur les cimes was the first of Delius's works ever to receive public per⁄ formance. It was given in Oslo on 10th October 1891 by Iver Holter when, under its Norwegian title of *Paa Vidderne*, it was described on the programme as a concert overture for large orchestra.[1] It was given again in Monte Carlo in February 1893, thanks to the support of Theodore and of Isidore de Lara. Delius had met de Lara through Strindberg and the occult. He was not only a dabbler in the unknown but a social lion, a great one with the ladies, and an artistic dilettante. He had even composed a few substantial works himself. Princess Alice of Monaco heard Delius's work when it was played and expressed great interest in it. She asked him to send her another of his compositions which he would like to be played but he ignored the offer completely. There were many which he would very much have liked to have heard but he was too proud to commit himself to a patron and far preferred freedom, in spite of the financial discomfort. *Sur les cimes* was not played again in his lifetime, nor did Princess Alice ever re⁄enter his life.

Two chamber works and a *Légende* for violin and orchestra followed a little later. It is not surprising that Delius felt inclined to write for the violin, because it was the one instrument which he played and under⁄ stood really well. Inspite of his proficiency, however, he gave up playing it at about this time.

In the autumn of this year Delius heard from his father's company secretary in confidence that Julius seemed to be sabotaging Max's efforts abroad and had removed all authority from him. The business was going downhill; would Frederick try to save the situation by intervening? Max was his favourite brother and the closest to him among the men in his family, but whether he wrote to his father is not known. It is somewhat unlikely because it is most improbable that Julius would have taken any advice or criticism from his renegade son. At all events Max left the family business and went to Canada.

Another reason for Delius's unwillingness to accept Princess Alice's

[1] Rachel Lowe, 'Delius's First Performance' (*Musical Times*, March 1965, pp. 190–2).

offer may well have been his preoccupation with another opera. This was *The Magic Fountain*, called in German *Der Wunderborn*.[1] At the end of 1895 it was accepted for performance at the German Opera House in Prague. But this good fortune was offset by bad; he had quarrelled with his uncle. The good old man had understandably become anxious at still having to support his nephew (and sometimes his nephew's friends as well), especially as he rejected the idea of composing anything 'com- mercial'. Theodore himself rejected commercialism for its own sake, but the idea of Frederick being at work on another opera that would quite likely end up unperformed in the same manner as the first struck him as nonsensical. He felt that it was high time he saw some return for his faith in his nephew and for his own substantial outlay in supporting him. To make matters worse, Julius had also become impatient and had reduced the allowance to Frederick by half, so that only £52 per annum now came from Bradford. Delius realized that he must look elsewhere for support and so turned towards Berlin, where his mother's sister-in-law Albertine lived. Her son Arthur, who got on well with his cousin, helped to persuade her that she must make it possible for the young composer to remain in Paris and this she did with some relish, for she could not bear any of the Deliuses.

Although it seemed that all was set for a performance of *The Magic Fountain* in Prague nothing further happened. The music had arrived there safely by Christmas 1895 and Sinding, who was in Prague, reported progress to Delius by letter. Professor Hutchings believes that Delius himself withdrew the opera, having had second thoughts about it and deciding that it must not be heard; alternatively it is possible that the committee of management in Prague decided at the last moment that such an unusual and unfamiliar work was too hazardous an enterprise for them. It is set in Florida and calls for exotic stage settings. Briefly the story is this:

Solano, captain of a becalmed Spanish ship (his name the same as that of the Delius orange grove) dreams about finding the Fountain of Youth. When

---

[1] A misapprehension has for some time been current about this opera as a result of its two titles. They are not two different works but the same one. It is still unperformed.

he prays for wind, the answering storm wrecks his ship. Watawa, an Indian princess, rescues him from the beach and falls in love with him. Against a lush swamp background they embrace, and the fountain is revealed. Watawa tries to keep him away, telling him that the water means death. When he invites her to drink with him, she rushes to drink before him and dies in his arms; in frantic grief he also goes to drink. The music shows a considerable advance over *Irmelin*, with passages of high mystery, charm and throbbing romance.[1]

Meanwhile, seemingly unconcerned, Delius was setting two songs of Verlaine, *Il pleure dans mon cœur* and *Le ciel est pardessus le toit*, which he scored for alternative piano or orchestral accompaniment. The latter is the preferable version, allowing as it does for far more subtleties beneath the voice. The Griegs continued to influence Delius and he regarded them both as his best friends, frequently sending them his compositions for their approval and comment. Grieg considered the three Shelley songs to be uncomfortably erotic and felt them to be reflections of Delius's life in Paris. Today one can take no such view of these songs, but there is more than a little in what Grieg said; for Delius was very often to be seen with women of one kind or another. It must be stated here, for a better understanding of his condition in later life, that at some time during the last five years of the nineteenth century he contracted syphilis in Paris. The disease was rife there. Gauguin also became a victim of it, in January 1895, while Renoir commented on it as a natural and commonplace ailment in a city where excitement and danger were sought in an almost desperate race to enjoy life to the full, no matter what the consequences might be.

I do not believe that Delius entered the race for stimulation in entirely this manner. It was probably sheer misfortune that caused him to bring upon himself the miseries of a then incurable disease, a social stigma (although few knew what was wrong with him) and a fearful bitterness. For he was scrupulous and fastidious in all things connected with his person.

[1] From an article by Denis Vaughan in *Opera News*, 29th December 1962.

CHAPTER III

1895–1901

IN THE quieter and more sophisticated society which Delius now tended to frequent he met a painter called Jelka Rosen. She had recently occupied lodgings in the Rue de la Grande Chaumière, opposite Mère Charlotte's, where she had often seen Delius in the company of his cronies: Gauguin, Slewinsky, Mucha, Strindberg and the *maître de ballet* of the Folies Bergères. The Rosen family were from Schleswig-Holstein and had a strict Prussian background. Jelka had actually been born in Serbia and was sent to Paris to paint, for she had real talent as a *pointilliste*. There she met Delius through Edvard Munch, the master of the 'graphic ara-besque'. Jelka was serious about her stay in Paris. She sought company and friends but was not there to find a husband, because men of her own age invariably bored her. She was fond of music and possessed a small but pure soprano voice. She had also just 'discovered' Nietzsche.

Round about Delius's thirty-fourth birthday in January 1896 he met Jelka socially (it is doubtful whether he even noticed her watching him from across the Rue de la Grande Chaumière). Their first topic of con-versation was their mutual respect and admiration for Grieg's music. But when Delius found that Jelka was at the time reading *Zarathustra* their conversation turned to Nietzsche, and her respect for his knowledge of the man and his teaching—which coincided with her own—led her to see in Delius something new and exciting that she had never seen in any man before. She wisely realized that he was likely to resent obvious attention and affection and that she must avoid showing any jealousy. There were plenty of occasions when she might have done so, for Delius, with his remarkably good looks, was seldom without female company and she was rather plain.

During the soirée at which Jelka and Delius met she sang two of Grieg's songs, and a day or two later Delius visited her in the Rue de Maine, taking with him a book of his own songs for her inspection. The one which appealed to her most—then and ever after—was *Twilight Fancies*, to words by Bjørnstjerne Bjørnson. They continued to meet and became close friends. They walked together when spring came and often ate late at Delius's apartment. Because he always composed at night and became fidgety when the meal was over, Jelka never tried to stay longer than she was wanted. It was perfectly clear to her at this early stage that music came first in their friendship; and her tact and understanding at a time when she wanted above all else to be with Delius showed that she loved him deeply.

In May her painting *Le dernier accord* was accepted for hanging in the Salon, and Delius gratified her enormously by his penetrating assessment of it. The picture is of a nude female figure seated, lyre in hand, in a land-scape with setting sun. Jelka had painted it in the garden of a house in the village of Grez-sur-Loing, near Fontainebleau. She was able to use this garden by permission of its owner, the Marquis de Carzeaux. The fact that it was overlooked by the presbytery next door, where the priest and several of his friends used to gather to enjoy the attributes of Jelka's naked models, was all understood and taken in good part.

For several months past Delius had been working on his third opera, *Koanga*. He had found a story called 'Bras-Coupé', a narrative within the novel *The Grandissimes* by George Washington Cable. It is a highly coloured story of the Creole society in Louisiana at the beginning of the nineteenth century, and instantly appealed to Delius, since he was familiar with its setting. 'Koanga' is a Congo word meaning 'arm' and is the name of the hero of the narrative: an African prince who by being sold into slavery in Louisiana is the arm cut off his tribe—the strong arm.

Delius had met an Englishman in Paris called Charles F. Keary who had been willing to adapt the story of Koanga and give it the necessary operatic treatment. Keary was an expert in Greek and Roman coins—more expert in this, one might think, than in making a libretto. But Delius appreciated his interest and accepted his achievement, entering into composition with the utmost confidence that it would be a huge success. Keary lived in the village of Bourron, only two miles from Grez, and this meant that Delius was able to combine work trips to his librettist with pleasure visits to Jelka. When Jelka was at Grez she stayed at its only hotel, the Chevillon, and there sometimes Keary and Delius joined her. They went for long walks *à trois* in the Fontainebleau forest, which comes down to within a mile from the edge of the village of Grez, until the whole area was well known to Delius. He was immensely taken with the village and its surroundings—as anybody is who visits it, even today—and confided to Jelka that this would be his ideal of a place in which to live and work: unspoiled, romantic, still. That he might eventually do so seemed impossible.

The summer of 1896 was spent at work on Act I of *Koanga*. Keary's adaptation, slightly at variance with the book, tells of the African voodoo prince, Koanga, who is sold into slavery and set to work for a Louisiana planter called Don José Martinez. The planter's wife has a mulatto half-sister, Palmyra, with whom Koanga falls in love. Jealousy intervenes in the character of Simon Perez, the overseer on the plantation whom Koanga kills before escaping into the forest. There he organizes a voodoo curse on everybody, in a vision hears Palmyra calling to him to return, does so and is treacherously killed. She stabs herself.

Koanga works so much better than *Irmelin* does on the stage that it shows a distinct advance in Delius's understanding of the medium of opera. The rich scoring and thick harmonies are most evocative of the plantation atmosphere and Delius has carefully cast his hero as a baritone; not only the masculine attributes of this voice but also its characteristics when the part is sung by a Negro add greatly to the total effect. It is very unlikely that Delius considered that there would ever be Negro singers available for the opera but he undoubtedly had Negro voices in mind when he wrote for Koanga and Palmyra. It is all very authentic. The introduction which frames the opera within an opera is a much more attractive start than that of *Irmelin* and once the story is under way we cannot help but be totally involved.

Simon Perez, the villain who tries to seduce his master's half-sister-in-law, is a despicable character and his predicament is interesting because dramatically it can lead to a variety of different endings. The arrival of Koanga, a new slave even though a prince of his tribe, is effective, and when Palmyra is given to him to make him obedient the action opens up into traditional operatic convention of ensemble, with each voice giving the character's own thoughts. At the beginning of the second act Perez learns that Palmyra is half-sister to Clotilda, who promises the girl to

BACK OF THE HOUSE AT GREZ TODAY

Perez providing he stops the marriage with Koanga. In the middle of the wedding ceremony in Act II Palmyra is dragged away by Perez, and Koanga in a blind rage assaults Don José, his master. At this point one is reminded of the scene in *Porgy and Bess* when Crown returns to Bess after the picnic: the excitement is intense and the solitary black man on the stage has a compelling primitiveness that is instantly effective.

The last act shows Koanga, the voodoo priest and other slaves who have escaped into the jungle exercising a voodoo spell with their own blood. This causes the slaves on the plantation, including Palmyra, to fall ill; but Don José has laid a trap, knowing that the male slaves must return if only for food. Koanga is aware of Palmyra's need for him and returns to kill Perez before he is himself cut down by hidden horsemen. As Palmyra stabs herself the story ends in yet more blood. Even though there is here a lowering of the dramatic standards which the relevant part of the original novel by Cable calls for, Delius and Keary omitted even more unpleasant details in an effort to make the work worthy of the opera house rather than a Grand Guignol.

Musically it is all well thought out, with a great number of touching, exciting or truly melodious moments. The Calinda scene in Act II, with its choral accompaniment by the Negroes (in French), has the strong whiff of authenticity, as in fact have all the choruses by the slaves. In choosing a subject which was familiar to him Delius was doing what Grieg had taught him, which was to use the folk melodies which he knew and build them into his music. Even if the audience did not know the originals, they would sound so well that they would be bound to come off effectively. Although Delius was not a native of Florida, his time spent there had allowed him to identify himself with the Negroes who had so recently been slaves and to make himself conscious of their feelings and their miserable lot. There can be few, if any, other operas which show such a mastery of an idiom into which the composer has not been born.

In August Delius went back to Norway for an unusual kind of visit. It was not so much a holiday this time as a musical tour that one might believe was all planned as a huge joke. He went in a group of three: with his Norwegian friend, the vagabond fiddler Halfdan Jebe, and Knut Hamsun. Jebe was a very good musician, and a humorist of the Rabelai‑

sian kind. This appealed very much to Delius's own sense of fun, although Jelka could never tolerate him. Hamsun was an author and on this occasion played practical jokes and also recited.[1] The trio toured small Norwegian villages, where Delius accompanied Jebe in duos and played Chopin solo and Hamsun chose most unsuitable poems to declaim. It is clear that the three artists cannot have been serious about their tour, nor can the places they visited have had much of an idea of the music they played—before or afterwards.

When Delius returned to Paris to continue his composition of *Koanga* he also devoted some of his time to sketching the Piano Concerto and making the basic plan of *Paris*. Florida was much on his mind, not only in connection with the opera which he was writing but also because he was contemplating a return to Solano Grove. Through the help of an American called Thrane, who was a property agent in Florida, he was considering leasing the grove for growing tobacco rather than fruit. Halfdan Jebe offered to accompany him there as friend and companion, particularly as he was curious to see the place which Delius had so often talked about. At Christmas time 1896 he told Jelka about his plan to go for a short visit to America. She was immensely upset, fearing as all lovers do that parting would bring forgetfulness. She was well aware that there were other women in Delius's life and was even more distraught when she heard that one in particular had publicly sworn that she would follow him all the way to America if necessary.

It may have been that pressing emotional entanglements had precipi- tated Delius's withdrawal from the Paris scene; or alternatively it has been suggested that he had a coloured mistress in Solano for whom he yearned. If such a Palmyra existed, and a fresh encounter with her would spur him to write the love music for *Koanga*, so much the better; if he had to shake off an unwanted female from Europe, he would be able to do that as well. So he and Jebe set off, and it was not until the ship was in mid-Atlantic that one of the passengers declared 'himself' as the young woman in Paris who refused to be parted from Delius. She travelled to Florida with him but there is no certainty as to whether they went *à deux* or whether the curious Jebe accompanied them. In either

---

[1] He was to win the Nobel Prize for literature in 1920.

event the journey seems to have had the required therapeutic effect on the lady, for she never came into Delius's life again.

News of the melodramatic disguise of her rival got back to Jelka, who now considered that she had lost Delius for ever. A rational mind tends to become irrational in love and to take the pessimistic view. Jelka busied herself as much as she could, determined to forget all about the fickle composer who had toyed with her feelings and then left her.

A surprising event caused her mind to be seriously diverted and occupied with other matters, so that had she wished to think only about Delius it is doubtful whether she would have had the capacity to so do. The Marquis whose garden she used as an open-air studio at Grez had been swindled out of a million francs and was desperately trying to raise as much as he could. He announced that he was selling all his estates in Grez-sur-Loing (of which the house and garden formed part) but that the amounts he required for the various properties must be handed over to him in cash at the time of signing the deeds. Jelka was determined to acquire the house and garden which she already loved so much, but by realizing her own investments and selling the lease of her flat in Paris she was able to raise only about half the sum required. Her mother, who used to stay with her at the Chevillon Hotel and knew Grez well, agreed to lend her the balance. Laden with banknotes, they both went down to the Marquis's château on the day of the sale, and shortly afterwards the Grez house belonged to Jelka and Frau Rosen.

Jelka moved in on 17th May 1897 with insufficient furniture and no money in her pocket. She sought the aid of servants in the village and organized a great cleaning campaign in the house and a weeding and tidying operation in the garden until the whole of her property was to her satisfaction. When the house was clean she found that she had got over the worst of the pain at losing Delius and was able to paint again. She invited a German friend called Ida Gerhardi to join her there and to bring her own furniture. Several other female friends used to go there at week-ends, even for weeks at a time. It was to be convent-like, Jelka decided—no more men.

Meanwhile in Florida Delius had been convinced that if he were able to buy the deeds of Solano Grove from his father he might well be assured of a steady income from tobacco, providing that he found the right kind of people to run the place for him. He certainly did not intend to do so himself. He returned to Paris at the end of June and to his surprise found that Jelka had left the Rue de Maine. He very much wanted to see her again and had no idea that his departure had caused her so much agony. He was given her forwarding address. A few days later a postcard came through the door of Jelka's new house, telling her that Delius would be arriving on the following day. Her state of mind can be imagined. There was no time to put him off—she did not even know where he was to be found in Paris—scarcely enough time to let the effect of the message take its full meaning. Delius arrived with the minimum of luggage and announced that he would be staying. Within a very short time Jelka gave up trying to resist the old feeling and resigned herself to the love for Delius which had never left her. She gave him a room to work in, complete with a piano, dispensed with her female friends—except for Ida Gerhardi, who stayed there for another six months in perfect harmony with them both—and let it be known to all artists in the district that Delius was back. From then on the house became a focal point for daytime parties, discussions, informal music and jollities of all sorts.

Delius was by now thirty-six years old, yet only one of his works had achieved a public performance. Considering the way in which his compositions were being finished only to remain on shelves to collect the dust, anyone less confident of his own genius and optimistic of an eventual recognition would have become most depressed. He did not even try to attract the interest of a publisher and seemed only to want to compose and to go on composing.

During the summer of 1897 he worked hard on the last act of *Koanga*, ministered to by Jelka and with the comfortable feeling that his librettist was close at hand all the time in the next village. Nevertheless he kept his apartment going in the Rue Ducoüédic and from time to time during the next seven years he went there for one purpose or another, never telling Jelka why or for how long he was going to be away. In spite of this she overlooked the humiliation she felt in such obvious infidelity and welcomed him back with open arms. When his visits to Paris continued, and as their own relationship became more intimate and intense, they had blazing arguments which always resulted in Delius going back to Paris, thus setting the cycle in motion once more. At such times Delius could be wickedly cruel and said things to Jelka that should never have been thought of, let alone expressed. He tried her sorely, yet when their sun shone over them and they were happy no two people could have been more blissfully content, no one person more sure that she was created to be the support of and comfort to this wonderful, sometimes horrible, but always remarkable genius.

The set of seven Danish songs dates from 1897 and includes *Irmelin Rose*, which is related to the opera *Irmelin* as well, as to a much later, independent work, the *Irmelin Prelude*. *In the Seraglio Garden* also belongs to this set and these two songs are among the finest that Delius wrote. That he should return to the Irmelin idea is strange, unless he intended to relate Jelka to the princess in the tower, waiting. Beside the Grez house is an old ruined tower called the Donjon in which, as local history has it, the mother of King François I died. Another legend states that an adulterous wife was shut up there to die; and, no doubt, like Irmelin she was forever gazing out of her cell across the River Loing to those very meadows which Jelka could see from her own garden. Delius was climbing about on the remains of the Donjon one day when he found a young jackdaw in its nest. He took it back to the house and called it Koanga. It became a member of the household and kept the magpies away, took instant and obvious dislike to certain visitors and—unlike the Jackdaw of Rheims—found and returned small objects which had been lost.

The year 1898 saw the main part of the work on a tone poem, at first called *La Ronde se déroule* (The Dance Goes On), which was to be subjected to a number of changes before Delius was satisfied with it. Even in the original version it was most exciting to hear and Delius had certainly mastered and fully harnessed the resources of a full orchestra to say exactly what he intended. Also one night he composed *Mitternachtslied Zarathustras* (The Night Song of Zarathustra) to words by Nietzsche. He was so excited by what he had achieved that he called out to Jelka and Ida Gerhardi, waking them and making them come down and listen. The work, for baritone, male chorus and orchestra, was later incorporated in the last movement of *A Mass of Life*. Delius also reworked several passages of *Appalachia* but this hung about until 1902.

In October his uncle Theodore suddenly died, bequeathing him a small sum of money—smaller, that is, than he had anticipated. Ten years of subsidizing Delius seems to have been taken into account. But spare cash could have come at no better moment. It enabled Delius to buy a Gauguin canvas. The artist had sent a new painting called *Nevermore* [1] from Tahiti to his friend and agent Georges–Daniel de Monfreid in Paris. Delius bought the picture for the absurdly small sum of 500 francs (£20) and hung it in his music room at Grez. It was his most cherished possession and it rapidly appreciated in value. In his will Theodore left a strange instruction, forbidding any servant or person other than a member of the Delius family to prepare his remains for burial. Delius performed the office of clothing his uncle's corpse in his evening dress and decorations, while the valet stood beside him, giving verbal instructions and passing the garments.

The fastidiousness and upper-class *hauteur* which his uncle possessed passed, in a manner of speaking, to Delius. Theodore was his only male friend of the older generation (apart from Grieg) and it was natural that Delius should regard him as a mentor more than his own father. It seems that he tended to imitate his uncle and that this trait was all the more obvious in his later life when it had become out-dated, when the expressions which he voiced were bordering on caricature. The arrangements for the funeral conflicted with a commission that Delius had accepted in the previous September. Gunnar Heiberg had arrived in Grez to ask whether he was prepared to write incidental music for his new satirical play *Folkeraadet* (Parliament), which was to be performed in Christiania (now Oslo) in the middle of October. He agreed but was diverted from the task and had little time to do more than map out the numbers until he heard what size of orchestra was at his disposal. Also his absence from the piano—where he always composed—put him at a complete disadvantage.

He sent the score to Heiberg and then went to Christiania for the première. He was warned when he arrived that there might be disturbances because of the play's anti-politician bias. There certainly were. The play was acted out with the utmost difficulty amongst an uproar that even included the firing of a blank cartridge. This drove Delius from

[1] *See* Appendix F, p. 162.

the theatre and across the road to the sanctuary of an hotel. Here he found the aged Ibsen—now over seventy—sitting alone, quietly drinking. After the first night the students who had been responsible for the uproar apologized and the play settled down to receptive audiences. Contrary to previous reports of this occasion, Delius did not conduct his score of *Folkeraadet.*

Before he left France for Norway Delius had heard from Dr Hans Haym, conductor of the Elberfeld [1] orchestra, that he was going to include *Over the Hills and Far Away* in early November; and so Delius called on him on his way home. It had been Ida Gerhardi who had effected an introduction between the two musicians—a fact that was to be of immense help to Delius over the next fifteen years. Dr Haym had prepared the piece well, so Delius thought, but the public was surprised by what they heard and did not react at all favourably towards it.

Delius was then working on the Piano Concerto, *Paris* and the revised *Appalachia*; and, spurred by the commission from Norway, he had started to send his manuscripts to the most likely German opera- and concert-conductors for their consideration. After some months had passed he had sent out so many scores to so many different places that it was often difficult to find where a particular manuscript might be, especially as in some cases they had been forwarded elsewhere at his request. One great disadvantage in Delius's working habits was his extremely small and lightly written notation—unlike his handwriting, which was on the large side and definite. Sometimes he even scored in pencil. No wonder that one conductor returned a very large-format score to him unread, with the comment 'optisch unmöglich' (impossible to read).

Delius returned to Grez for two weeks after the Elberfeld concert and then went to Paris where he played a four-handed arrangement, with Henry Falke, of his new Piano Concerto. Falke, who took the solo part, was a celebrated pianist who had recently become established, yet this did not save the day. The audience was unsympathetic to the whole en- deavour, which is perhaps why, after this and subsequent performances, Delius recast the conventionally shaped work into the one continuous movement which we know today.

[1] Elberfeld is now part of the town of Wuppertal in the Ruhr.

43

At Christmas Delius and Jebe went to England together and spent a week with Delius's favourite sister Clare, now married and living near the Yorkshire village of Lothersdale. Delius took the complete score of *Koanga* with him and played through the opera to his relatives. While he was in England he decided to make arrangements for a concert of his own music in London. Since nobody else seemed to wish to do so he would be his own promoter and find out two things: firstly, exactly how several of his unplayed works would sound; and secondly, how an audience of inquiring and paying members of a general musical public would react to hearing them. Keary had told him about a concert agency which was reputed to be the best in London. It was called the Concorde Concert Control (C.C.C.) and had an idealist in its managing director, Norman Concorde. When Concorde heard that Delius had three unperformed operas already written he tried to interest him in the formation of a permanent opera in London, but Delius was very soon unimpressed with the idea, particularly as he had no money to put into it, and brought Concorde back to his original idea of a concert.

He was anxious that Henry Wood should conduct his works, but in the end it was Alfred Hertz from Elberfeld, with an *ad hoc* chorus and orchestra and a specially engaged leader—Halfdan Jebe. The concert was given at St James's Hall on 30th May 1899 and consisted of:

Part I Fantasia for Orchestra, *Over the Hills and Far Away.*
　　　Légende for violin (John Dunn) and orchestra.
　　　Folkeraadet: 3rd and 4th movements from the suite.
　　　5 Danish Songs sung by Christianne Andray with orchestral accompaniment: 'Through long, long years'
　　　　　　　　　　　　'Let Springtime come'
　　　　　　　　　　　　'Irmelin Rose'
　　　　　　　　　　　　'On the Seashore'
　　　　　　　　　　　　'Wine Roses'
　　　La Ronde se déroule.
　　　Mitternachtslied for baritone (Douglas Powell), men's chorus and orchestra—from Nietzsche's *Zarathustra.*
Part II Excerpts from *Koanga:*
　　　Prelude to Act III.
　　　Quintet and Finale of Act I.

Act II complete.
(Soloists: Ella Russell, Tilly Koenen, G. A. Vanderbeek,
William Llewellyn and Andrew Black).

Concorde had done his job well, for the advertising was satisfactory and
the right members of the press had been invited. But his estimates of the
cost were far from accurate.

The music itself was received politely and with some surprise. The
audience was mystified by the new idiom, so different from their usual
fare of Wagner; and several of the reputable critics were actually at a loss
as to know what to say. They first took up several inches in explaining
who Delius was—a very necessary expedient. The shortest comment of all
seems to have come from Julius Delius, sitting at home in Bradford and
keeping well clear of St James's Hall. On the following morning he read
his *Yorkshire Post* carefully while his children sat round the table in
silence, waiting for him to tell them about the concert. He avoided the
subject entirely throughout breakfast but on getting up from the table
remarked casually: 'I see Fritz has given a concert.' That was all.

Delius was satisfied that his musical intentions had been properly interpreted and that what he had envisaged had also come off, generally
speaking, very well. It was a complete musical education for him to be
able to hear his own works. But when the bill came he was horrified to find
that the cost to him was £500 and not the £200 which was Concorde's
debit estimate.[1] Delius never forgot this error in calculation and lapsed
into silence whenever Concorde's name was mentioned; in all fairness,
however, it must be stated that orchestral rehearsals had had to be increased
in number owing to the unfamiliarity of the players with this kind of
music, and the orchestra also had been increased from seventy-five to
ninety. Also, owing to the illegibility of some of the scores, extra
assistance in copying was unavoidable. No one came forward to help
Delius with his obligations to Concorde, and plans for a second concert
to help recoup losses were abandoned. Delius was forced to dip into his
own pocket and part with the last of his uncle's legacy.

[1] Considering that the 1899 pound sterling had about ten times the
purchasing power of the 1971 pound, the comparative figures are £5,000 and
£2,000—horrifying indeed.

He returned to Grez financially chastened but musically uplifted by the experience and finished the composition of his *Paris: A Nocturne* (The Song of a Great City). For once the theme was neither the countryside nor Nature but how well he knew Paris. Three sub-headings from his sketches of the work are:

Scènes parisiennes
L'Heure de l'absinthe
Heureux rencontre

which give a rough idea of the piece. From the opening on the bass clarinet, through the romance and gaiety, it is a wonderful—if somewhat Germanic—impression of Paris. The French have never taken to this portrayal of their metropolis, nor, for that matter, to any of Delius's music. Perhaps it is the German influence which they find too heavy, though the delicacy and wistfulness which they so admire in Debussy is not so far away.

Paris calls for a large orchestra including quadruple woodwind (apart from the flutes) and two extra horns but, since Delius hardly ever begins louder than *p*, these reserves are kept back until they achieve a major impact on the listener. The opening might seem to be an ominous sonority but when heard it is a relaxed, magical sound. Three bars later the oboe introduces a theme made up of several groups of three quavers. This motif is exploited throughout and might be called the signature of *Paris*:

Ex. 1

Although Delius had not been able to wrest the deeds of Solano Grove from his father, they had come to an arrangement whereby Thrane had leased it for tobacco-growing. But now there was depressing news from Thrane. There had been devastating changes in the climate throughout Florida and people who had gone there for health reasons had been obliged to leave. A great deal of the area round Solano was deserted and overgrown and no longer such an attractive proposition to specu-lators or planters. In 1899, however, Delius found two American brothers who were willing to take over the estate; but after they had been there for only a short time, and had borrowed from Delius as well, they disappeared completely, leaving the place deserted. After this additional financial disappointment, and not having his uncle to go to for help any longer, Delius was in a poor situation and in a gloomy frame of mind. He did what was best in the circumstances and concentrated on a new work.

This was to be his fourth and best-loved opera. The year 1900 was spent in getting the libretto into shape; the original story, called *The People of Seldwyla*, was by the Swiss author Gottfried Keller. Delius called his opera *A Village Romeo and Juliet* (in German it is *Romeo und Julia auf dem Dorfe*) and determined to get away from the conventional shape of acts by setting the work in a large number of short scenes which he called 'pictures'. He turned once more to Keary for help but soon found that his friend's efforts were of little merit. Bearing in mind that the German market was a better proposition than the English one he asked Jelka to translate Keary's poor English into good German, which she did with some considerable success. The English version in use is yet another translation from Jelka's German.[1]

The only available score nowadays is the one published by Harmonie Verlag in 1910 and with a few small changes this is the performing score of the opera. An earlier edition, dated 1907, of which there is a copy in the British Museum, has an unexpected difference. Delius withdrew this edition because he had had a most important afterthought, the motif.:

Ex. 2

which occurs time and time again in connection with the two lovers.

[1] See the interesting articles in *Opera*, April and May 1962, and the note in the June 1962 issue, p. 418.

A Village Romeo and Juliet has been likened in spirit to *Tristan und Isolde* in so far as the lovers are resigned to death, which means a new life elsewhere. Wagner's and Delius's views on death differed somewhat, but even so this is not the whole meaning behind the Delius opera. What gives it that strange and (once more since *Irmelin*) fairy-tale characteristic is its construction by means of short 'pictures' rather than whole acts, making the action more plastic and the music continuous, since so many of the scenes are linked together by a short interlude. This is so close to Debussy's plan in *Pelléas and Mélisande* that distinct similarities between the two works cannot be overlooked. One such likeness is the virtual impracticability of arranging excerpts; yet Delius left the longish inter-lude called 'The Walk to the Paradise Garden' as an introduction for the general public who, because of it, are probably more aware of this opera than of *Pélleas*, in which Debussy wrote nothing that can be extracted.

The only possibly weak aspect of *A Village Romeo and Juliet* lies in the prologue, set six years before the rest of the opera. This had worked very well in *Koanga* where the prologue and the short epilogue were set in no specific place or time; from the dramatic point of view this opera can stand perfectly well without either of them. But in *A Village Romeo* we have a slight jolt before gliding into the important part of the story and the most beautiful and effective part of the opera.

The fairground scene which immediately precedes 'The Walk to the Paradise Garden' is one instance of Delius almost succeeding in writing a parody of cheap merry-making and popular songs of a transitory nature, as opposed to folksongs. Because of this rumbustious atmosphere the 'Walk' benefits enormously in performance by setting off and reducing to musical tinsel the previous scene—something which does not happen when the interlude is taken out of its context.

The characters of the lovers are of a simple purity. Their parents and the people at the fair are of little account; it is the Dark Fiddler who is the musical and dramatic foil to Sali and Vreli (or Vrenchen, as Delius called her). He and his music defy categorization: whenever he appears the action stands on tiptoe, so fey and unusual does he seem. But since it is not made at all clear in what relationship he stands to Sali and Vreli, whether as a guardian, a tormentor, or merely as a means of securing their release from an unsatisfactory existence, his comings and going seem more and more to be on a different plane from that of any other character in the opera.

The total achievement of this opera is considerable: it is without question Delius's supreme composition for the stage. The last duet of the lovers (tinged with Shelley in its words 'See the moonbeams kiss the woods, the fields and all the flowers') is so utterly poignant when set against the immediate double-suicide which follows that one is surprised at Delius's seeming knowledge of the power of death.

The Germanization of the names of Delius's compositions, such as *Lebenstanz*, was, in the same context as the translation of the new opera, good commercial sense. But whereas Delius called himself Fritz until 1903, he was Frederick afterwards—a curious contradiction.

One notices at this time a strain in his relationship with Jelka. Probably she felt that it was high time they married; but he was still jealous of his independence and insisted on retaining it—and his Paris flat—for as long as possible. The situation at Grez suited him perfectly, and we must not deceive ourselves into thinking that he was anything but self-centred. An artist's life is such an isolated one that he is often likely to be an ego-centric. Once that tight little knot that is himself is allowed to unwind and wholly to embrace other people all the time, he becomes artistically flabby and less efficient. His mind must work as his inspiration dictates, and this can only happen when he is as far as possible untrammelled by others. Jelka found a way out of her unhappiness by entering into an extended and affectionate correspondence with the sculptor Rodin.[1] He was not only an admirer of her paintings but was touched and warmed by her attention and response. For a short time he received some of the love that Delius seemed to be shunning.

At the end of 1900, a worrying year, Delius met two young Germans—again through the help of Ida Gerhardi—and between the pair of them they put up £500 for the lease of the Solano Grove plantation, less the house and a piece of ground round it. They arrived there at the beginning

[1] Thirty-five letters from Jelka to Rodin are in the Rodin Museum in Paris; seventeen written by Rodin to Jelka are in the possession of the Delius Trust. The correspondence began in October 1900 and ended in April 1914, so far as is known. It has been documented and annotated by Lionel Carley.

of 1901 and at first all went well. But in the spring a small tornado ruined the young tobacco shoots and once more desolation reigned.

The year 1901 was a peaceful and industrious one for Delius, who finished the composition of *A Village Romeo and Juliet*. He was not only enriched by the £500 but still mentally fortified by the experience of hearing so much of his own music in London. The faithful Haym gave *Paris* its première in Elberfeld and Delius dedicated the work to him. Busoni promised to give a performance of the Piano Concerto in Berlin and Delius went there to discuss details with him. Busoni at that time enjoyed the organized attention at his house of a large number of female friends, like a salon, and Delius found himself entirely unable to pin him down. The date of performance was put back several times until in the end it was postponed indefinitely. Having wasted over two weeks in Berlin Delius went back to Grez, nursing a resentment against Busoni. This was not helped when, a little later, Busoni performed *Paris* so appallingly badly that Delius is reported to have gone white in the face and walked out of the concert hall without a word to anybody.[1] From now on Busoni and Concorde were together in Delius's bad books.

Before he finished *A Village Romeo and Juliet* he had already made great strides with a new work called *Sea-Drift*, for baritone solo, chorus and orchestra. Almost for the first time he found that sheer inspiration was guiding him and he had merely to write down the notes as they came into his head. This deeply touching composition, inspired by the words of the American poet Walt Whitman, will be discussed later.

In October 1901 Julius Delius died at the age of eighty. Even after Frederick's undoubted artistic success with the 1899 concert in London and later on the Continent he had not made the slightest move to acknowledge his son's progress in music. Nor had he offered any *rapprochement*, apart from yielding up the Solano Grove lease in the previous year. There was very little left of the formerly prosperous family business, and to crown all Frederick was not mentioned in the will. True he received some £550 from the residual estate but once again this was

---

[1] At this concert Sibelius conducted the first German performance of his *En Saga*, but the whole evening was called a fiasco by the critics, with *Paris* coming in for especially harsh words.

far less than he had been hoping for. With Theodore dead, his aunt Albertine unapproachable for any more funds and no other Delius caring to help, there was only one direction in which he knew he might look. Only one person continued to have unbounded confidence in him and in his work, was prepared to feed, help and house him and actively to participate in his work when asked to do so. This was Jelka.

How Delius felt about his obligation is hard to tell. We do not know whether there were yet any signs of the disease which was later to strike him down; probably at this time it was merely dormant. The artist in him took all this easily and philosophically but the man of the world and nephew of Theodore found it difficult, even shaming. Contrariwise, the artist in him was reluctant to commit himself to a binding contract; yet he had to eat. The inward struggle was a difficult one and Delius did not come out of it unscathed. In his biography [1] Sir Thomas Beecham says that at this time and onwards, when Delius was suffering this change of temperament, 'the iron was in his soul'. This is a severe indictment which he makes no attempt to explain.

Delius was more serious because he was working harder. He was less cheerful possibly because of the concern about his health, especially with regard to Jelka. He was more remote and aloof and intolerant of mankind the more he shut himself up in Grez. People do not have iron in their souls without good reason. Delius's severe personal crisis left him with a new attitude of mind and a new capacity for music. Hard work helped to keep him on an even keel—work and the ever present understanding of Jelka. For her the correspondence with Rodin was the palliative, so that the difficult months passed and gave way to something quite different, though long expected.

[1] *Delius* (1959).

CHAPTER IV

1902-10

EARLY in 1902, with *A Village Romeo and Juliet* behind him, Delius embarked on the composition of another opera, but in entirely novel circumstances. Ricordi of Milan had recently decided to imitate their publishing rivals Sonzogno by holding a competition for a one-act opera of an hour's duration. The Sonzogno competition of 1890 had been won in a blaze of glory by Pietro Mascagni with his *Cavalleria Rusticana*.

Delius entered into the spirit of the Ricordi enterprise rather too much in the same manner as they had done, in sheer emulation. The Mascagni style, blood and thunder, was far removed from his own, yet he chose for his subject a melodramatic little piece called *Margot la Rouge*. The libretto was supplied by Rosenval.[1] The story tells of a soldier returning to Paris from the wars to find his fiancée offering herself for hire in a café. The soldier, Thibault, is killed in a fight by Margot's latest admirer, called simply the Artist, whom she in turn kills; she is then taken away by the *gendarmerie*. There is no literary merit in the story and little musical merit in the score. Delius was out of his element in trying to write like Mascagni, but there was enough powerful thought behind the score for some of it to be salvaged and effectively used in another composition over a quarter of a century later. *Margot la Rouge* was issued in a lithographed edition in vocal score with the piano accompaniment arranged by Ravel. Hence it is not always possible to know what Delius's orchestration was

[1] The lithographed score states that the words are by Rosenval, which would seem to indicate that the librettist was a man; but in the Archives of the Delius Trust there is a letter, written in French and signed 'Rosenval', in which all the adjectives referring to the writer have unmistakable feminine agreements. As far as I know this is the only evidence to support the theory that the librettist was a woman.

FREDERICK AND JELKA DELIUS, *c.* 1919

like. The three-quaver phrase from *Paris* constantly appears (see Ex. 1, p. 46). Despite the failure of this departure from his usual style, *Margot la Rouge* had left him with a taste for melodrama, and he looked seriously at Oscar Wilde's *Salome* in terms of another one-act opera. He discussed the idea with the poet's executors in London, Wilde having died in Paris two years before. But while he was still toying with the subject, Richard Strauss obtained the rights for himself.

In 1903 Delius's engagement to Jelka Rosen was announced. This had long been expected, but Delius seems for several years to have been unable to resolve his conflicting emotions. It would be unfair to suppose that he was now forced into matrimony; but with his father dead there was real need for a replacement in the way of a father-figure, if not a father-mother figure. Delius had no god, his uncle had gone and now his true father as well. Thus he was wholly reliant on Jelka.

The ceremony, a civil one only, took place at six o'clock on the evening of 28th September 1903 and was performed by Charles Girbal, assistant to the Mayor of Grez. The register reads: 'Fritz Théodore Albert Delius, compositeur de musique, âgé de 41 ans domicilé en cette commune avec Hélène Sophie Emilie Rosen, artiste peintre âgée de 31 ans domicilée à Grez-sur-Loing, née à Belgrade (Serbie) 18 décembre nouveau style (30 décembre ancien style) 1868.' The witnesses were René Besse, the carpenter who lived immediately opposite the house; Isidore Roger, the gardener; and Marie Blandel, the Breton cook who could not write and so was unable to sign the register. No one else was present. It was a village wedding but not a true French village wedding because the parish priest was not there. Delius's family responded to the event in different ways. His mother sent him £25, much to his great surprise, while his aunt Albertine expressed her doubts as to whether her eccentric nephew was wise to embark upon married life until he had won a 'secure position'. Mme Rosen's contribution was more generous than the first and certainly more practical than the second, for she made over the Grez house entirely to her daughter, rent free, and cancelled all interest payments on her side of the loan. It was now Jelka's house. Delius gave up, at long last, his flat in the Rue Ducoüédic and henceforth his one and only address was Grez-sur-Loing, Seine-et-Marne (the house never had a name).

With his marriage Delius's fortunes seemed to take a turn for the better. *Nachtlied Zarathustras* was given at the Basel Festival, while *Koanga* was scheduled for production at Elberfeld during the following season. The new intendant at the Elberfeld Opera was the brilliant Hans Gregor (later to be Director of the Berlin Komische Oper and the Vienna Opera) and the new chief conductor was Fritz Cassirer, a great admirer of Delius's music. Hans Haym at the Elberfeld Concert Hall continued to champion his works as before.

We have seen that Delius and Strauss were simultaneously interested in *Salome* as an opera. These two composers were contemporaries in the German music scene of 1904; their personalities and music, however, were entirely different. Delius was the refined, the delicate, the economical in composition; Strauss was rich and beefy, often vulgar, a profligate in construction and in sound. They were the Eusebius and Florestan of early twentieth-century music. Strauss was well established after his *Salome* and Delius was not yet established at all, yet Strauss was already suffering from the criticism that he had had his last word—a criticism that followed him throughout his life—whilst Delius in 1904 was a novel element, a strange and often unpalatable one in music, and had a slight advantage over his colleague in that his expression was new, unfamiliar and he could never be accused of having run dry. The centre of anti-nationalist German composition, which rested in Delius as Strauss's opponent, was in Elberfeld, championed by Hans Haym, Julius Buths, Gregor and Cassirer, though Strauss conducted there too.

Delius and Jelka went to Elberfeld for the production of *Koanga* in March 1904 at the Stadttheater. They arrived to take part in the final rehearsals; Jelka had designed one of the sets, and Delius conducted several rehearsal sessions. His sister Clare (Mrs Black) was living temporarily in Bonn (at that time a quiet little town on the Rhine associated only with Beethoven) so that her children might learn to speak German fluently, and she went over to Elberfeld to see her brother again and to meet his wife for the first time. The American baritone Clarence Whitehill sang Koanga and Rose Kaiser was the Palmyra. They both contributed effectively to the great success of the opera under Cassirer's direction, which captured the spirit of the music and transmitted it to the players and singers. Gregor's staging was said to have been expert too, and the singers had been well cast and well rehearsed. Yet it was not in the same category of opera composition as Strauss's works; for when one compares the structure and libretto of *Koanga* with its contemporary *Salome*, or even with Strauss's earlier *Feuersnot*, there is little doubt that the Bavarian was in every way master of this form.

In May the revised *Appalachia* was performed by Haym in Elberfeld. In its final form it shows a stylish hand and it would be all the more interest-ing to be able to compare this version with the earlier one. As we know it, the work comprises a set of variations, but with a difference. The theme on which they are based is saved until the end so that when it arrives we feel we know it intimately. But until we do hear the theme—an old slave song sung by baritone solo and chorus—and understand it we are not properly aware that *Appalachia* is about the American slaving days, of the same period in American history as *Koanga*. It is a tragic little song, telling of the plight of slaves who might suddenly be sold to another planter and be forced to leave their families and go to another place to work—the situation which has given currency to the expression 'sold down the river'. This grim theme is sandwiched between softer ones of optimism but never of expectation.

The main theme is introduced *a cappella* by the chorus (though the harmonies are essentially Delian rather than plantation). Considering that this is the first composition in which he used a full orchestra and chorus, it is a remarkable demonstration of his personal idiom in these terms, and of the most delicate instrumental colouring, although it is the second (1902) version of the work which is heard today.

When Delius returned to Grez, satisfied and a little wiser, he found a letter from Henry Wood saying that he wished to include the *Lebenstanz* in a Promenade Concert during August 1905. The manuscript parts were somewhere in Europe and Delius had to search far and wide among the many conductors on his list who received new works. Eventually Wood grew impatient and decided to postpone giving the work in London, so when Delius found the parts he sent them to Julius Buths in Düsseldorf. Buths, without further ado, performed the *Lebenstanz* at the end of 1904. Meanwhile, following the success of *Appalachia*, Haym gave the Piano Concerto there with Buths as soloist.

Fritz Cassirer was becoming a close friend and in August he and

Delius went on a bicycling tour of Brittany. Delius benefited enormously from the keen and well-stocked mind of his companion, who was the ideal person to help him with an idea which had been simmering for some time. He had been pondering how he might set Nietzsche's *Also sprach Zarathustra*, the monumental, metaphysical and mystic work which had inflamed the whole of Germany either in admiration or detestation of the pagan ideals which it contains. It is certainly a masterpiece of thought, and Delius's interest in it stemmed from a long association with the book rather than from the wish to rival Strauss's tone poem, so named, which had come out in 1896. Cassirer, in whom Delius confided, saw it all perfectly clearly. The composer must not try to formulate a pro-gramme, for none exists in the poem. He must match the mood of it in his music by selecting sections to set; and, if Delius agreed, Cassirer was prepared to select them. From this holiday in Brittany the *Mass of Life* was first conceived and when Delius returned to Grez in September he had a ready-made text to set to music.

Cassirer's fertile mind was engaged with Gregor's at this time on another large-scale plan, though one which concerned bricks and mortar rather than musical notes. They intended to open an entirely new opera house in Berlin on the lines of the Opéra Comique in Paris. Because every town in Germany had its own opera house this scheme was not as outrageous as it may appear nor as unwelcome to the general public as Concorde's half-baked ideas for London had been in 1899. The new house was going to be called the Komische Oper and it would present Delius's *A Village Romeo and Juliet* during the first season. Cassirer and Gregor collected the necessary support for their giant enterprise, and while the building was in progress they started to recruit management, orchestra, singers and staff.

In December 1904 *Paris* was given in Brussels, but the performance was not appreciated and did not lead to repetition of his works there for many years. Delius ignored the event and set himself to work on the *Mass of Life* and on recasting the Piano Concerto into its final one-movement form. He hoped that the new opera house might provide him with a secure stage for his operas. The new Berlin opera house opened its doors on 18th November 1905 with a performance of Offenbach's *Tales of Hoffmann*. It seated 1,250 people and was built in the modern baroque

style.[1] It operated on the *stagione* system so as to attract maximum atten-
dances. Cassirer's plan for staging the Delius opera in the first season
failed to materialize, and *Die Fledermaus* and *Lakmé* were given instead;
but *A Village Romeo and Juliet* was promised for the winter season of
1906–7.

The year 1906 opened for Delius with a performance of *Sea-Drift*
in Essen. This put before the German public a work which caught
its imagination and started the vogue for his music in that country,
bringing him into the front rank of composers who were in demand. Yet
this performance might have failed if Delius had not been there to make
sure his instructions were observed. The local conductor, one Georg
Witte, had recruited his chorus from the town and had engaged a baritone called Josef Loritz. At rehearsals the chorus had been puzzled by
Delius's harmonies and together with Witte they had made alterations to
their parts, not believing that what was printed was what the composer
really intended. Also, what the composer intended was in most instances
far more difficult to sing. Delius flew into a rage when he heard them at a
late rehearsal; prompted by Haym to take a temperate line, he instructed
them firmly to sing exactly what he had asked. When they did so and
were joined by the orchestra, Witte realized that the smallest alterations in
a single voice had radically upset the harmonic effect.

The success of this performance led to pamphlets about Delius and his
music being circulated in Germany and, more important still, an
approach to him by the publishing firm Harmonie of Berlin. This firm
had already achieved a name for their elegant scores which had carried off
prizes for design and print and which were the responsibility of Harmonie's active director, Alexander Jadassohn. Jadassohn had grown to
like Delius's music and at once made plans to publish *Sea-Drift*, the
Piano Concerto and *Appalachia*.

Sea-Drift is indisputably one of Delius's finest works. He had never
before attempted to portray the sea in music, but in this opening [2] the
flute and oboe leave us in no doubt:

[1] The Komische Oper is in the Eastern Sector of Berlin, having survived
the Second World War.
[2] Arnold Bax used the same idea in his *Garden of Fand* (1916).

Delius

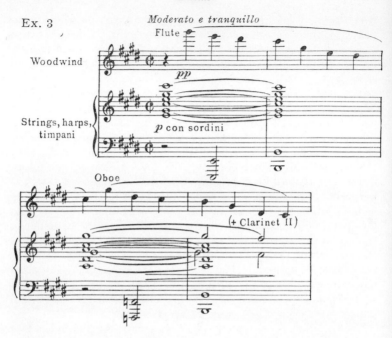

Ex. 3

The story is told partly by the chorus and partly by a baritone who adopts the characters of a boy and two sea birds. This may sound curious, so expressed, but the gulls, who are the main protagonists in the story, very soon occupy our attention as if they were human. The boy finds a

Ex. 4

gull's nest and watches the two parent birds sitting by turns on their clutch. One day the hen flies off and never returns, while her mate is left alone and exhausted, calling for her while he dutifully remains on the eggs. It is all so hauntingly clothed in music that it seems a heart-rending tragedy between two human beings. In this short fragment (Ex. 4, p. 58) we seem to be involved in one of the greatest love stories ever told.

Sea-Drift was dedicated to Max von Schillings, intendant of the Berlin State Opera and a very influential man.

Delius was planning to go to Norway as usual when he received a report that Grieg was dying. Grieg sent a message that he was too ill to see anybody, although he had recently been greatly cheered by a new friend called Percy Grainger. Grainger was an Australian musician of powerful talent, then twenty-four years old, who had been educated in Germany and had made the acquaintance of Grieg in London. He was an exceptional pianist and had been inspired by the Norwegian com-poser to study folksong. Later Delius was to be equally uplifted by Grainger's ebullience and humour. Sir Thomas Beecham draws our attention to the fact that these three musicians were united not only in friendship but in their attitude to folk music. Grieg's music was based on the Scandinavian folk heritage; Delius used the Negro melodies of Florida and lesser Norwegian ones; while Grainger was an inveterate collector of hereditary tunes, no matter where from.

Delius did in fact see Grieg in Norway that summer, though for the last time. He spent his working hours there on the *Songs of Sunset* for mezzo-soprano, baritone, chorus and orchestra, to poems by Ernest Dowson. He extracted one poem that is known as 'Cynara' [1] and set it as a separate work for baritone and orchestra, feeling that its subject needed no chorus. Jelka did not accompany him to Norway that year but stayed at Grez to complete several paintings that she was intending to show at the Independent Painters' Exhibition in Paris. They both visited the metro-polis in September to see a retrospective exhibition of Gauguin's paint-ings and sculptures at the Salon d'Automne in which *Nevermore* was on loan among the 227 exhibits.

In October Cassirer reported to Delius that Gregor was being in-

---

[1] The poem's full title is *non sum qualis eram bonae sub regno cynarae.*

fluenced against a production of *A Village Romeo and Juliet*, although earlier difficulties in finding a suitable tenor had been resolved. At last a committee, consisting of the opera's business manager, the producer, a prominent Berlin agent, the critic Max Chop and two cousins of Cassirer's all sat down to listen to Cassirer play through the score on the piano. They argued all night but in the early morning it was agreed that the opera was a fine work and might be produced provided that certain alterations were made to the score. In their opinion a spoken prologue before the first act was also entirely necessary to set the scene and explain what the opera was about. The première was fixed for January 1907. It actually took place on 21st February. Delius had agreed to most of the wishes of the committee but even so Max Chop's criticism was less than polite, according to Philip Heseltine,[1] who assumes that the performance was 'a grisly affair' in which only Cassirer and the orchestra came any-where near the mark. But as a first night is not necessarily representative of a run of performances Beecham believes that the total effect did Delius no harm.

It is important to place *A Village Romeo and Juliet* and its score in relation to the staging and atmosphere which the opera demands. The one outweighs the other, so that a large orchestra and a larger than usual orchestra pit is demanded for a work that depends on an intimate theatre to gain maximum effect. These two requirements seldom go together and they remain one of the problems of any production of the opera.

Delius stayed in Berlin after the end of the season and then accom-panied the opera company to London, where they were due to give a few weeks' performances at the Adelphi Theatre of *The Tales of Hoffmann*. The Komische Oper was not at all enthusiastically received, however, and the run was brought to a sudden mid-week end, so ruining any hopes which Delius might have had of hearing his own opera performed there. He remained in London for over a month and renewed old friendships with John Coates, who introduced him to the Savage Club; with Henry Wood; and with the composer Cyril Scott. Through Scott Delius met Norman O'Neill and his wife and this was a great friendship that lasted all their lives. He met many other people in London, mainly

[1] The first English biographer of Delius (1923).

artists and musicians, and went back to Grez greatly cheered by his impressions of 'the dozen or so budding English composers'.

The compositions in progress were the first *Dance Rhapsody* and *Brigg Fair*. The latter is a set of variations. The instrumentation is masterly and the immense orchestral climax never ceases to be exciting, just as the work continues to yield fresh beauties with every hearing (see pp. 112–20).

In September Delius returned to London to hear Henry Wood give the Piano Concerto at Queen's Hall with Theodor Szántó (to whom it is dedicated) as soloist. Cassirer was at the concert, developing ideas about giving one or two Delius works in London himself. Despite the failure of the Komische Oper he was deluded into believing that London was capable of sustaining more music than was available at the time and in any case felt that the city was a likely one to assist in the advancement of his own career as conductor. He had already planned in his mind his first concert, which would include Delius's *Appalachia* and Strauss's *Ein Heldenleben*. Delius was naturally interested in these proposals, but even if he was sceptical he said nothing. He agreed to help Cassirer to find a suitable orchestra in London, and while trying to decide between the relative virtues of the Queen's Hall Orchestra and the London Symphony he found that there was another which he knew nothing about. This was the New Symphony Orchestra, which both Beecham and Wood have claimed some part in supporting in its early stages.[1] Delius went round to see Beecham and expressed his desire to engage the New Symphony Orchestra on Cassirer's behalf. Beecham had heard of Delius but had never seen him, nor had he imagined that he would find himself face to face with the composer in London. He records that his first reaction was one of great surprise (unusual for Beecham) and that he kept on saying to himself: 'He must be a cardinal or at least a bishop in mufti!'[2] He was amenable to Delius's suggestion and arranged for the orchestra to be available towards the end of November.

Cassirer's concert took place on 22nd November. Clare Black records that she regarded it as the most important day in her brother's life.

---

[1] As Sir Henry Wood never mentions Sir Thomas Beecham at all in his autobiography and Beecham only refers to Wood in passing in his two books, it is perhaps better to let the matter rest.

[2] *A Mingled Chime* (1944).

It may have been, but not for the same reason as she thought. Beecham also regarded it as the most important day in his life because he heard *Appalachia* and was henceforth to become one of the principal champions of Delius's music; more than that, he was to be Delius's editor, a musical position which badly needed filling. The programme of Cassirer's concert consisted of the *Meistersinger* Overture, *Appalachia* and, 'after a proper interval', as *The Times* critic thought fit, 'the dance from Strauss's *Salome* performed, as need hardly be said, for the first time in London'. This work took the place of *Ein Heldenleben*, because Strauss was anxious for as many performances of his *Salome* music as possible. Of the com' poser of *Appalachia*, *The Times* critic said : 'He has much to learn before he can be held to be a successful or an effective composer of choral music.' Perhaps this critic was disturbed at seeing the chorus resting until the last movement, save for their few 'La's'. The most useful criticisms came from Robin Legge (formerly of Leipzig), now writing for the *Daily Telegraph*, while Norman O'Neill contributed the effective programme note.

Delius stayed with the O'Neills in Pembroke Villas, Kensington; Norman and Adine O'Neill both became his and Jelka's firm friends, so that whenever the Deliuses were in London it was understood that they must stay with them. O'Neill was a prolific composer who achieved his greatest successes in the field of light incidental music for plays. His scores for *The Blue Bird*, *Mary Rose*, *The Pretenders*, *The Prisoner of Zenda* and seven of Shakespeare's plays give some idea of his versatility. He also wrote many songs and orchestral pieces. It was undoubtedly O'Neill who persauded Delius to accept the vice'presidency of the Musical League, with Henry Wood, Granville Bantock, Percy Pitt and others under the presidency of Edward Elgar. At this time it was under general discussion only and no doubt was chewed over unmercifully at the O'Neill's, where Beecham, Cyril Scott and Balfour Gardiner were frequently to be found. The conversations in this corner of London proved to be very stimulating to Delius.

Meanwhile in early September Grieg had died. Although Delius had been expecting the news he was much upset when it reached him. Grieg had been an important influence in his life, in encouraging him in the early days, in convincing Julius to allow him to go on with his music and also in stimulating his interest in Norway and its folksong.

Beecham was anxious to perform works by Delius in London during the early part of 1908 and had especially *Paris* and *Appalachia* in mind. He had been able to discuss the latter work with Delius in London but wished to find out more about the composer's intentions regarding *Paris*, which he had never heard. He invited himself to Grez at the end of 1907 with the specific purpose of asking a number of questions about this work. This would have been necessary even if the score had been marked with dynamic directions; but none of Delius's scores ever indicated many nuances or even broad outlines of expression or of interpretation—he seemed to expect his music to speak for itself, which it seldom does. As it turned out, Delius was of no help at all. He may have been unable to help Beecham, for he made certain that the two of them were never alone together long enough for the subject to be raised. In the end Beecham returned to London to work out his own version of *Paris* and from this time onwards his editions of Delius's scores have been accepted as authentic.

London heard *Paris* under Beecham's baton at Queen's Hall in early 1908 and *Appalachia* again in April. A few weeks before that Delius had conducted *Appalachia* himself in Hanley, showing himself to be entirely unable to project his intentions to the orchestra. He seemed all the time to be swallowed up in the enjoyment of his own composition, identifying himself with it in completely the wrong way, so that this came between him and the players. It was very seldom afterwards that he took the baton in his own hand. He returned to Grez from England to work on his next opera. He had finished the *Mass of Life* and had carefully prepared a new text to set. It was to be called *Fennimore and Gerda* and was based on a novel by J. P. Jacobsen called *Niels Lyhne*. Lyhne is the name of the somewhat doubtful hero, while Fennimore and Gerda are the two women in his life. There are eleven scenes in the opera, of which nine make up the Fennimore part and the last two are the Gerda end of the story. It may be assumed that Delius found this formula of 'pictures' a satisfactory one, but in pursuing it for this opera he was not employing it quite in the same way as he had done in *A Village Romeo and Juliet*, which was one continuous story.

The orchestral piece known as the Intermezzo from *Fennimore and Gerda* is the best-known part of the work. It is made out of the interludes before the two Gerda scenes and the last four bars of Gerda. There is thus no Fennimore in it. To hear the opera in performance reveals initially interesting characters who are not developed during the course of the work. Delius seems wrapped in deep thought (like Fennimore herself); and while his score is magical and beautiful it seldom touches the emotions of the characters and does little to help balance the curious construction of the end of the opera, with the tiny Gerda episode in which the lonely hero finds love at last. It seems a pity that these two fragments from Jacobsen's carefully constructed story were not more skilfully extracted, for there is much else in the book which would have made a plot that jars less than Delius's version. The difficulties involved in staging and playing the opera have helped to consign it to near oblivion— an unfortunate state of affairs which the few performances it has had have failed to reverse.

Apart from the London and Hanley performances in 1908, Basel had given *Brigg Fair* successfully in February and now the Munich Ton- künstlerfest presented the second part of the *Mass of Life*. Two French critics who were at the performance likened Delius to Debussy, but only in so far as a Delius-Weber Debussy-Wagner relationship. They also regretted that the whole of the *Mass* had not been given rather than such trifling works as a *Flagellantenzug* of Karl Bleyle. Delius did not go to Munich but stayed in Grez, at work on the *Songs of Sunset* for a mezzo- soprano with a very high range, baritone and orchestra. He also wrote the glorious *In a Summer Garden*, a companion piece in musical character to *Brigg Fair* and breathing the very air of Grez. It is dedicated to Jelka with Rossetti's words:

> All are my blooms and all sweet blooms of love,
> To thee I gave while spring and summer sang.

As it exists in published form it is one of Delius's masterpieces, perfectly formed and devoid of many of his clichés. It shows how much surer he was becoming in finding a musical form that fitted the subject, and reference to a score of the first version of *In a Summer Garden* [1] will

---

[1] There is one in the possession of the Delius Trust with some of Delius's reworkings on it; there is also a clean score in the BBC Music Library, copied from MS. parts in 1942.

indicate precisely how second thoughts were preferable in the case of this composition. The little figure of four semiquavers which occurs through-out the woodwind from bar six and onwards in the familiar version is altogether absent in such predominance; there is now a better transition from the first section to the second and the ending is completely changed. The whole form of the work is greatly improved, and while the earlier version may still be playable there is no doubt that the final one is a masterpiece. Form still tended to elude him more than melodic or harmonic elements in his composition, and it is often stated that the inner parts of Delius's works appear to have no line and that true polyphonic writing is absent. This is true if one applies this style of composition to Delius but in fact one should not do so. His style is different because texturally he moves from one chord to another, linking each with a melody so that harmonic freedom is at once evident. It is arguable whether the chordal progressions or the melody came first into his mind, but it must still explain why there is no genuine polyphony and why the whole structure is impaired if a single note is altered.

Delius had enthusiastically welcomed the attention of the music publishers Harmonie Verlag, and had agreed to let them act on his behalf. At first they seemed efficient and reliable. But in April 1909 he experienced great difficulties with them. They were not only employing an appallingly bad translator for English texts without any reference to him but they were charging exorbitantly high sums for the hire of parts in England. This was effected through the London office of Breitkopf and Härtel, who seemed to delight in putting difficulties in the way of would-be performers instead of encouraging them. Delius sought the advice of Beecham, who called in William Wallace, a highly cultured literary and musical person who had recently made a skilful translation of Strauss's opera *Feuersnot* for Beecham. Wallace agreed to tackle Harmonie, and built up a case against them, after which he was able to quote chapter and verse of their faults and to ridicule their pigheadedness. He also discovered that one of the texts (Nietzsche's) was not in copyright, and advised Delius to take a firm stand against Harmonie. Delius accepted Wallace's advice and commenced legal proceedings against his own publishers, a most uncomfortable and worrying state of affairs for him.

On 10th June 1909 Beecham gave the first performance of the

whole of the *Mass of Life* at Queen's Hall. It was at the end of this concert, he recalls, that a member of the audience audibly informed a companion that the name of the chorus-master was Nietzsche.

In the autumn of 1909 the complete *Mass of Life* was performed in Elberfeld under the direction of Hans Haym, followed by a spate of per-formances in England of earlier works; *Sea-Drift* was given in Sheffield with Frederic Austin as soloist and Wood conducting, and there were further performances under Beecham in Hanley and again the next day in Manchester.

Beecham was by now thoroughly taken with all of Delius's works, and was warming to the idea of starting a permanent opera company in London, although he must have known of Concorde's failure as well as the more recent Komische Oper disaster. With a small part of the Beecham Pills fortune that was at his disposal he broke fresh ground with plans for a most varied and intelligently compiled repertory of operas, and booked Covent Garden for a season in early 1910, before the Inter-national Season was due to begin. The conductors were to be Bruno Walter, Percy Pitt and Beecham himself, and the operas would include the British premières of Strauss's *Elektra* and Delius's *A Village Romeo and Juliet*. The Strauss work turned out to be a *succès fou* and rather stole press interest, which could have been spread more evenly among the other works. It also drew more than its fair share of the public, so that one planned performance of *A Village Romeo and Juliet* was replaced by *Elektra*, leaving only two in the season. At the première there was a reasonably good house and Delius, who was present, received kind applause when he appeared on the stage at the end. But the second per-formance attracted a very poor audience and the opera did the worst business of the season. The two other English offerings of Beecham's season—Ethel Smyth's *The Wreckers* and Sullivan's *Ivanhoe*—are markedly inferior works; yet one can understand that the style of Delius's opera was far removed from anything that had been heard in London opera houses before. At the same time it is true that Covent Garden is far too big a house for the work, and it is scarcely hindsight to say that it was bound to fail.

Unfortunately the immediate advent of Diaghilev and his rich and luxurious productions was the worst thing that could have happened to

Delius so far as London was concerned. Nothing could have been more at variance with the immediate furore which Diaghilev was to cause than the quiet and peaceful scores which Delius was saving up for presentation. The new vogue demanded a new look and a new sound. From this point of view Delius might as well return to the nineteenth century and stay there.

Naturally Delius was angry and jealous of Diaghilev's success, especially as the Russian impresario was being helped by Beecham, whom for a while Delius felt had deserted him at a critical moment. He expressed his feelings in a spiteful diatribe—one of his very few appearances in print—in *The Sackbut*, a magazine edited by Heseltine. Edwin Evans and Ernest Newman came in for a slanging, but more especially did 'Dixie, Dalcroze, Duncan and Diaghilev—they are all manifestations of the same thing . . .'.

The year 1910 was the end of an era on the London stage: the last year before the appearance there of Diaghilev and his Ballets Russes and Russian opera. They had already been seen in Paris in 1909 and were to burst upon London in 1911. They raised the standard of perfection from the accepted norm in all they did, so that even the Beecham fortune was unequal to Diaghilev's seemingly bottomless purse. The fact that there was no purse there and that Diaghilev existed by borrowing and begging is beside the point. In any case it is certain that British methods of stage production in 1910 were obsolete, dull, uninspired and in need of an enormous transfusion of colour and energy. Despite his own protestations to the contrary, there is strong argument that Beecham's sense of staging, although technically assured, was artistically wanting. There are many photographs in existence that show not only what he was content to put up with but what he boasted about and which, by today's standards, are dreadful, even allowing for changes in fashion. There is no evidence that Delius was better served in Germany.

While Beecham concentrated on the musical side of things Delius was beginning to air his professional grievances publicly; he ranted and raved about the state of affairs in English music. He declared that they were in the hands of incompetents and that music was far better served abroad—a not unknown line for expatriates to take on all sorts of subjects. This no doubt surprised his friends, who had always found him affable, if somewhat over-cynical and hypercritical of others. The cause of this most probably lay in his state of health, which began to deteriorate while he was in London in 1910. He was suffering from stomach pains and serious twinges in the back and was in a highly nervous condition. He had finished scoring *Fennimore and Gerda*, so for the moment there was no need for him to concentrate on a major work. He was certainly far more intolerant and irascible from now on and until the last years in Grez, but it is not certain whether this was caused by the disease which was permeating his body or whether the disease was made worse by his own nervous state. At all events 1910 marked the beginning of his gradual decline in health.

The Musical League's Festival, arranged for the summer, had been cancelled—the last event planned for this undistinguished and unfortu-nate organization. Like Concorde's ideal of an opera before and Beecham's League of Opera afterwards the Musical League was out of step with the times. Nobody with money, save the few exceptions like the Beechams, the Courtaulds and Lady Cunard, backed opera for its own sake. There was enough music in London for the ordinary, apathetic concert-goer. It was bound to fail. Delius had devoted a good deal of time to it and whatever he had hoped for in so far as performances of his works were concerned had failed to materialize. Furthermore he was considerably irked by the requests that had been made for his appearance at committee meetings in London when he considered that correspon-dence would suffice. He for one was not displeased when the Musical League died a quiet, unmarked death.

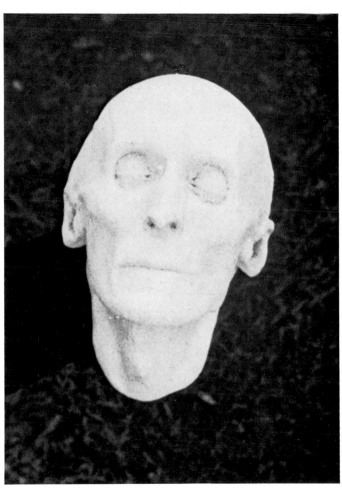

DELIUS'S DEATH-MASK

CHAPTER V

1910–THE END—AND AFTER

IN 1910 an Eton schoolboy called Philip Heseltine heard a performance of Delius's *On Craig Ddu* and was instantly bowled over by its sound. The work, for unaccompanied chorus, was first given at Blackpool in 1910. Hence Heseltine may have heard the first London performance. He was sixteen years old and determined to hear as much of Delius's music as he was able. That summer he went to France to spend a holiday with his uncle, Arthur Heseltine—known as 'Joe'. He was an eccentric, an indifferent painter and lived in the village of Marlotte outside Paris. Philip was astonished to find that not only is Marlotte within two miles of Grez-sur-Loing where Delius lived but that his uncle already knew him. And so a remarkable and in some ways unfortunate friendship started and grew between the two—remarkable because of the intense pleasure it gave to Delius and unfortunate because of Heseltine's particular psychology.

Philip Heseltine was extremely talented in all sorts of direction and as Peter Warlock, the composer, he possessed a knowledge of Tudor music second to none. His own songs are touched with genius and he could have been brilliant in any one of several ways had he been less of a dilettante and had he exercised himself more than he did. His correspondence with Delius shows that he sought and was given advice by entirely the wrong person and that Delius was unaware—until too late—of the kind of person Heseltine really was. Delius treated him as though they both possessed the same characteristics and gave him the same warnings that he would have wished for in his own youth. But they were not in any way comparable either as personalities or as occupiers of the same environments, and Delius's advice did irreparable damage.

At the end of 1910 Delius's physical condition had deteriorated even further and his tour of sanatoriums began in a search for a successful cure. In March 1911 Jelka told the O'Neills that he was looking much better after Wiesbaden and that he was able to go for walks; but he was thin and haggard, though working hard and correcting proofs of the *Songs of Sunset*. The song cycle to Dowson's words had a German text which Jelka had made after much difficulty. The work was performed at Queen's Hall under Beecham in June and Delius went there to hear it. Otherwise he stayed in Grez for the whole year.

The strange and somewhat sinister work *Arabesk* (which Delius always wrote as 'Arabesque') was a product of 1911. It is a setting for baritone, chorus and orchestra of J. P. Jacobsen's poem about Pan and it should be heard in the original Danish to achieve its full effect. Delius's fondness for Jacobsen's poems continued to yield material for setting, as had already happened with *Fennimore and Gerda*. *Lebenstanz* underwent its last revision during this same year and *Summer Night on the River* was composed. Between 1911 and 1912 Delius wrote *The Song of the High Hills* for chorus and orchestra, the longest of his 'tone poems'. The high hills refer to Norway and the piece has a certain bleakness about it, as if Delius's own warmth was being sapped away. This is even truer of the *North Country Sketches*—a reference to Yorkshire—where the movement called 'Winter' sparkles icy cold in such an intense manner that for sheer imagery it is unique among Delius's output. With the return to 'Spring' the set ends in more familiar temperatures. *North Country Sketches* was dedicated to the conductor Albert Coates and is in four movements: 'Autumn (the wind soughs [1] in the trees); Winter Landscape; Dance; The March of Spring (Woodlands, Meadows and silent Moors)'. The opening of the work gives way to a luscious tune on the cellos.

In the second movement Delius gets his effect of extreme cold by dividing the upper strings (see Ex. 5, p. 71).

Completely contrasted with the *North Country Sketches* is *On hearing the first Cuckoo in Spring*. There is scarcely a composition by Delius better able to help dispel the idea that he was hardening his musical voice. The cuckoo in this French spring is undoubtedly from the garden at Grez (he is represented by the clarinet in the orchestra). The work is built on two themes, the first of which sounds very much

---

[1] Sough: to make a rushing, rustling or murmuring noise (*O.E.D.*).

Ex. 5   *Very sustained*

like the kind of English folk-tune used in *Brigg Fair*; the second is Norwgian.[1]

The Birmingham Festival of 1912 turned out to be the last of its kind, with two full concerts on each of three days: 1st, 2nd and 3rd October. After *Elijah* on the morning of 1st October, the evening concert started with the *Coriolan* Overture, Brandenburg Concerto No. 3 and Liszt's first Piano Concerto (Rosenthal), all conducted by Henry Wood. After the interval Elgar conducted his *Music Makers* and Sibelius his Fourth Symphony. Delius was present but did not introduce himself to Elgar and Elgar in turn avoided Delius. On the last day, after *Messiah* in the morning, the evening concert consisted of Verdi's *Requiem*, *Sea-Drift*

---

[1] See p. 102.

with Thorpe Bates as soloist, and Wotan's Farewell from *Die Walküre*. Again Henry Wood conducted both in the morning and the evening and Clarence Whitehill sang in *Messiah*, Verdi's *Requiem* and as Wotan. *Sea-Drift* was considered far less difficult and obscure than it had been in the previous year.

After the festival Delius visited his mother, who had moved to Windsor some time after the death of Julius. His aunt Albertine had recently died and had left him a substantial sum, so he may well have wanted to make sure that his mother was cared for. At all events he never saw her again. Certainly she needed no longer chafe at him for his 'precarious' profession, for he and Jelka were now fairly comfortably off, thanks to royalties. Characteristically, Jelka's anti-British feeling and Delius's bitterness about England caused them to buy stock in Germany, America, anywhere but in the land from which there would have been no difficulties over collecting dividends or realizing capital, since Delius always retained his nationality. The summer holiday was spent in Italy; Delius found Venice particularly to his liking. He met an American sculptor there called Henry Clews, who was to be a close friend for the next twenty years.

The Delius-Heseltine correspondence was at its peak. Delius was advising the young man to resist parental wishes in the direction of the Civil Service. It is revealing to find that no matter where he was, or how busy, he always found the time to write to Heseltine. He knew only too well what it was like to be without help from anybody, and this fondness for the young man served to place him *in loco parentis*. But the vigour of youth and the excitement of growing up deluded Heseltine into imagining that half-hearted effort was sufficient. He also thought, misguidedly, that he 'knew it all' and that he was going to be welcome wherever he chose to go. True he had a quick and lively pen, a talent for musical research and arranging and a feeling (rather than a leaning) towards the theatre. Had he received strong direction and firm discipline at this time of his life, so that he might have become really proficient in one of the many untrained skills which he exhibited, his premature death at the age of thirty-six might have been averted.

The year 1914 began with spring weather in January—a misleading forecast for the year that was to change everybody's way of life and thought more radically than ever before. On 20th January at a Royal Philharmonic Concert the Dutch conductor Willem Mengelberg gave the *First Cuckoo* and *Summer Night on the River* for the first time. Delius came to London for this event and returned to Grez during the summer. He and Jelka stayed with the O'Neills as usual and saw many of their friends. They were happy and it looked as if the bad times were behind them now. Less than a month after their return home, on 4th August, World War I began its four-year course.

After the first German advance at the end of August most French people were convinced that there was no hope for them and this premonition of disaster affected even Grez-sur-Loing and its inhabitants. Delius wrote a long letter to Norman O'Neill, telling him of the dreadful sights he saw. because Grez was on one of the main north-south axes for the evacuation of wounded, and the British Army under General French had their headquarters at Fontainebleau, the Deliuses thought it would be advisable for them to leave the district in case a battle came to be fought there. There was also some pressure from within because Joe Heseltine was spreading rumours that Delius and his wife were spies; one evening a crowd collected outside the house, calling on Delius to come out. Stones were thrown and only when Delius failed to respond did the crowd disband. Delius and Jelka buried about a thousand bottles of wine in a natural cave in the garden, concealed the entrance to it (which was not difficult) and then removed their most precious paintings from the walls. *Nevermore*, a picture by Munch, and two by Jelka were taken from their frames and rolled up, especial care being paid to *Nevermore*. They then caught the train to Orléans.

After a miserable journey they settled down to rest and to eat surprisingly good food, glad of the opportunity to feel hunted no longer. When the German advance was stopped for the time being they returned to Grez to resume their old form of life. It is interesting to find from a descriptive letter to O'Neill how much Delius modified his views on England and the English. He shows great respect for the way in which their soldiers behaved and organized themselves, but he spoke in a very different voice about the enemy: 'If the Germans will only get rid of their café concert Kaiser and his numerous family, and become a peaceable nation once more, I think there will be no more war in Europe ever again. But they've got to be smashed first—and the sooner the better.' [1]

The war affected Delius far more deeply than he had imagined possible. The Germans regarded the English declaration of war on them as the worst kind of treachery and from that moment there was an intense national hatred of everything and everybody English. This was extended to Delius, despite his parenthood, and that he spoke fluent German and was married to a Prussian wife. Richter referred to him at Bayreuth as 'unser Delius' (our Delius) but this attitude was not reflected in Germany at large and no more of his music was played there until after 1918. In consequence all German royalties ceased and, because a large proportion of his wealth was invested in Germany too, Delius suffered a great financial loss which made itself cruelly felt by the end of 1915.

He then decided to go to England. Because the cross-Channel steamers were not interfered with by the Germans, the journey presented no difficulty. He and Jelka stayed near London for almost a year, first with Beecham in Watford and then at the Woods's. He arrived in England in a highly nervous state but began to settle down and work on his *Requiem*. This is a large-scale composition dedicated to all young artists who lost their lives in the war, yet it has a distinctly anti-Christian bias. Sir Thomas Beecham evinced a dislike for the work on these grounds and he never performed it. In view of the fact that there is invariably a return to deeper religious feeling in wartime, the thought behind the *Requiem* was curiously out of step with the current attitude.

The work calls for extra woodwind (in particular the lower instruments), six horns and extended percussion, as well as the usual instrumentation, double chorus and soprano and baritone soloists. The words, which Delius seems to have taken and slightly changed from Shakespeare, Nietzsche and also the Bible, offer contradictory sentiments which, puzzling as they appear today, over half a century ago must have been entirely incomprehensible in their calculated cynicism. Several performances of the work have been given in England since 1965, and now that a score of the work is available it is seen to yield felicities and delicate touches of orchestration together with complete control of the

[1] Derek Hudson, *Norman O'Neill—A Life of Music* (1945).

large orchestral and choral forces. The *Requiem* is not a dark work, for it glorifies life and urges the full use of it, for 'they die, and ne'er come back again'. Delius's belief in a superior Being, neither the God of Isaac, nor Jesus Christ, nor Mohammed, nor Allah, is seen when he sets *Hallelujah* against *Allah il Allah*. This is what he called 'the great laws of All-Being' and it offers the key to the understanding of the *Requiem*—and of Delius. He described the work as follows:

It is not a religious work. Its underlying belief is that of a pantheism that insists on the reality of life. It preaches that human life is like a day in the existence of the world, subject to the great laws of All-Being. The weakling is weighed down thereby and revels in magic pictures of a cheerful existence hereafter. The storm of reality destroys the golden dream-palaces, and the inexorable cry resounds, 'You are the creature of the day and must perish'. The world tries to soothe the fear of death; 'the highways of the world give birth to gods and idols'. The proud spirit casts off the yoke of superstition, for it knows that death puts an end to all life, and therefore fulfilment can be sought and found only in life itself. No judgment as to doing and not doing good and evil can be found in any ordinance from without, but only in the conscience of man himself. Often a man is judged worthless to the world and its laws, who should be exalted by praise for his human goodness, and the love of which he freely gives. Thus independence and self-reliance are the marks of a man who is great and free. He will look forward to his death with high courage in his soul, in proud solitude, in harmony with nature and the ever-recurrent, sonorous rhythm of birth and death.

Delius and Jelka were back again in Grez before the end of 1916. They had pined for their home and had not enjoyed living in England. Jelka wrote to the O'Neills lamenting that the garden was full of weeds and the pump was broken, but saying that they were much happier, and Delius had settled down again to his work and was engaged on a substantial composition called *Eventyr*. The idea came to him from a Norwegian fairy-tale by Asbjørnsen (the title means 'Once upon a time'). In size of orchestral demands, in length and in skill of orchestration it can be compared with a Strauss tone poem. It may be sombre, and it is certainly rarely heard, but it is an excellent piece that is really descriptive of its title and abounds in harmonies and atmosphere that conjure up to perfection the crooked little men of Norse mythology. It also possesses the unusual and most effective touch of two shouts by a small male chorus. Delius was also revising parts of the *Arabesk*, a work that is very similar in feeling to *Eventyr*—both Scandinavian in their roots, both dark in texture and in spirit. But financial burdens were pressing on him and he cursed the war and especially those responsible for it. After his first flush of English patriotism his old egocentricity returned and he regarded the whole state of affairs as a personal affront.

The O'Neills had a daughter born to them in early 1916 and Delius asked them—to their great surprise—whether he might stand as godfather. He showed his usual devotion to children by personally choosing and sending the little girl a golden necklace. This cannot be interpreted as a change in religious feelings but merely as a desire to please the people who had always been so kind to him and to Jelka whenever they were in London.

A change had come over Delius's form of composition as the war years continued. In 1916 and 1917 for the very first time he cast several works in the classical moulds which he had always despised before. These were two concertos (one for violin and another for violin and cello), a string quartet and a violin sonata. Meanwhile the correspondence with Heseltine continued unabated. Delius gave advice in connection with the young man's latest ideas about forming an opera company in London which was going to have 'no compromise with the mob'. They would perform *A Village Romeo and Juliet* without scenery. Although this was entirely contrary to the spirit of the work, as well as to Delius's own intentions and directions whenever the opera came to be performed, both before and after, he nevertheless agreed with Heseltine that his idea was best. Perhaps he was tired of the young man, perhaps Heseltine was tiresomely insistent on agreement. Needless to say the plan failed to materialize and Heseltine merely annoyed everybody he spoke to about his schemes, Beecham in particular. They were much too far-fetched and removed from hard bargaining, hard cash and the box office.

By the end of 1917 Delius found that he had to move away from Grez again and he resolved to return to England until the war was over. Once again he was far too exposed to the enemy for comfort, and the fear of being overrun was too much to risk. He was also starved of music. What concerts there were in Paris did not appeal to him and there was none anywhere else. So again he and Jelka hid their wine, rolled up the precious canvases and arrived in England on 30th September. Henry Wood met them and took them to his house where Delius, having safely arrived indoors, took from inside his trousers the complete score of *Eventyr*, written entirely in pencil. At that time codes in musical notation were being used and to have declared his composition to the Customs on landing would certainly have meant its confiscation.

Disturbing news from Grez upset him even more in 1918. The house had been used as a French officers' mess and it was said to have been left in a foul state. Jelka volunteered to go back there and inspect the damage, for the news had caused Delius to say: 'The house is spoilt for me for ever and we shall try to sell it as quickly as possible.' Of course this was only the first reaction to a personal insult by strangers, and when Jelka arrived she found that a great deal had already been done to restore the house to its former shape and to return looted property. In November 1918, with the war over, Delius decided to apply himself to getting his works performed again, all over Europe if possible. During the war Beecham had had control of an opera company and of the (old) Royal Philharmonic Orchestra. He had lost no opportunities to champion Delius. On two occasions he had given the fifth scene from *A Village Romeo and Juliet* (the Fair, ending with 'The Walk to the Paradise Garden' interlude), in preparation for his proposed revival of the whole opera after the armistice.

Delius had been for a cure to Biarritz. He then went on to Norway for the first time in four years. While there he heard the best news of any, which was that the opera house at Frankfurt-am-Main was contemplating a production of *Fennimore and Gerda*. If this happened it would indicate that he had been re-established in Germany; the first production of an opera now nearly ten years old would help to make amends for his wartime oblivion. But his funds were still frozen in Germany and that affected him most, for as time went on the Deutschmark lost value, crumbled and finally collapsed, and his former wealth was lost to him. Although he had other investments in America it was some time before these were released.

Between the end of the war and the production of the opera in October 1919 several important performances of Delius's wartime compositions were given. The first of these was at the Wigmore Hall in November, immediately after the armistice, when Beatrice Harrison gave an impassioned performance of the Sonata for Cello and Piano, accompanied by Evlyn Howard-Jones. She was one of the celebrated Harrison sisters; daughters of an army officer, they had spent their early life in India where they had learned what it means to command.

The Cello Sonata was dedicated to Beatrice Harrison. It is in one movement and shows an advancement in understanding of the instrument's capacity over the earlier Double Concerto. But it is an arduous work to play since there is hardly a single bar's rest from beginning to end. This is characteristic of Delius. He becomes so intoxicated by the effect of a theme that he does not pause to consider whether the performer needs also to pause for breath or wind or to rest aching muscles. The pressing urgency for a good editor of Delius's scores was obvious. In January 1920 a promising young conductor called Adrian Boult gave the first performance of the Violin Concerto at a Philharmonic Concert, with Albert Sammons as soloist. Of all the concertos this is by far the most successful because Delius was a violinist and was perfectly at home with the instrument and its capabilities. But the work is not in the repertory of as many great violinists as it should be because it lacks the bravura finish which is calculated to inspire applause. In his usual manner of letting the ending of a work die away, Delius leaves the soloist high and dry on a *pianissimo*, though this is not a valid reason for so few performances. There are criticisms that it rambles on and that if the 'best' parts were put together and a shorter work formed it would become more viable. But when one gets to know the Violin Concerto well it is inconceivable that it can ever be heard in another form.

The Double Concerto shows Delius less at home with the larger instrument, whose accompanying passage-work tends to dawdle along. It needs two soloists of great competence if the total effect is to emerge as equal partners and orchestra, rather than a violin concerto with an obbligato solo cello. It was first performed in January 1920 at Queen's Hall under Sir Henry Wood, with Beatrice Harrison and her sister May as soloists. The String Quartet and *Eventyr* were both performed in 1919 in London, the first by the London String Quartet, and the second by Wood and the Queen's Hall Orchestra. All this should have pleased

Delius considerably, but he seemed less than grateful, and both he and Jelka were difficult guests, longing to get back to France and away from England.

At the same time as the Double Concerto was played in London, Delius and Jelka were there again for *A Village Romeo* at Covent Garden. Miriam Licette was the Vreli, Walter Hyde the Sali and Percy Heming sang the Black Fiddler. Sir Thomas Beecham comments on the occasion: 'The composer seems to have been satisfied with the produc٬ tion and the performance, for neither he nor anyone else was found to utter a serious word of complaint about it.' Beecham adds that the company which performed the opera had achieved a great sense of unity and ensemble because they had been together for five years. Two unac٬ companied choruses *To be sung of a summer night on the water* were given in the same month of January 1920 by Charles Kennedy Scott and the Oriana Madrigal Society. Delius attended only the opening per٬ formance of the opera on 19th March and returned to Grez on the following day.

Had he stayed a few days longer he would have made unnecessary the journey to Grez of the London impresario Basil Dean. Dean had been fortunate enough to acquire from Beerbohm Tree, to whom it had been offered but who could not be bothered with it, a manuscript play called *Hassan, or the Golden Journey to Samarkand* by the poet James Elroy Flecker (1884–1915). Uncut, it was far too long; but Dean saw at once that it could be made into a lovely vehicle for the stage and that it was going to need a very special kind of incidental music. He approached Ravel, who declined the offer, and then had no ideas at all until March. He was walking down Bow Street in the evening when he saw that an opera by Delius was being performed there. He went in and arrived in his box at the moment when the interlude called 'The Walk to the Paradise Garden' was being played. He understood there and then that this was the composer for *Hassan*, and had to chase after Delius in order to talk to him about it.

Delius was delighted at the prospect of working in the theatre again and accepted the commission eagerly. Dean left him with a copy of the acting version of *Hassan* and the cues marked in it, saying that his pro٬ duction was scheduled for 1921 at His Majesty's Theatre. But it did not materialize during that year because of an official limitation on spending: it would have been an inauspicious moment to mount a lavish production.

During 1921 Delius began to lose the use of his hands and by the end of the year he was paralysed in both of them. He and Jelka spent their summer holiday of 1922 in Norway, where they owned a chalet built to their specifications. Throughout July and August he improved to the extent of being able to walk with two sticks, but he was fast becoming a helpless invalid. To make matters worse, Jelka was not at all experienced in taking musical dictation and Delius had fresh thoughts longing to be released from his mind and committed to paper. Because he was now unable to write at all Jelka took over all the business correspondence, badgering managements and their friends to try and encourage performances. All this while Delius fretted and became very difficult to live with because the mind within the diseased body was unimpaired. Among the friends who visited him at Grez in 1922 was Beecham, who noticed what a fearful change had come over the invalid. In the following year, when he was taking a cure at Bad Oeynhausen near Hanover, his sister Clare failed to recognize him because he had become so shrunken and lifeless. Suddenly, within less than twelve months, the man had become the myth that he was to remain for the next fourteen years, imprisoned inside a decaying body that spent most of the time in a wheel-chair.

The two Hungarian composers Béla Bartók and Zoltán Kodály were among Delius's friends. From time to time Bartók sought his advice on a number of technical points; he obviously valued Delius's opinion, for he also sent the completed compositions for his comments. Both Bartók and Kodály were particularly interested in Delius's wordless choruses, which they considered to be unique in conception. The two composers first became acquainted with Delius over a matter of copyright; if their works were published without the name of a non-Hungarian on the scores, they were instantly pirated in America, because neither Hungary nor Russia were signatories of the Berne Convention. Delius agreed to have his name added as a 'reviser' and treated the whole matter, as they did, as a huge joke.

Another, more substantial, friend was the one-time companion of Grieg, Percy Grainger, who, although known to Delius for some years, now appeared on the scene as a real companion and source of fun and mischief, which helped to take Delius's mind off himself. Grainger, born in Australia, had become an infant prodigy pianist. He deputized for Grieg at Queen's Hall and learned from him how important the folksongs of any nation are to its musical heritage. He was one of the first to collect them with the aid of a gramophone and his acknowledgments and essays on all his arrangements of folk-tunes are models of originality and scholarship. In 1914 he came to England, but he was already international in outlook and did not truly belong to any one place; in this respect he resembled Delius. He was as fond of practical jokes as anybody, and he used to make Delius laugh until it was painful for him to continue, by throwing a tennis ball over the roof of the Grez house from the garden and running through the archway to catch it before it landed in the street outside. He frequently took Delius for walks, pushing the wheel-chair at a great pace along the roads and down the garden, with Delius calling him to stop, yet enjoying it all the time. There was a need for a few people like Grainger, able to stand up to Delius and turn his increasing sourness into good humour by either ignoring him or teasing him until the real nature of the man emerged again. When Delius was alone with Jelka he had time to ruminate on his misery and often made life nearly unbearable for her.

Because *Hassan* had been postponed in London other theatres sought permission to perform it. Darmstadt gave the world première (in German) with Frederick Valk as Hassan. The London production opened on 20th September 1923 and ran for 281 performances. It had an exceptional cast, with Henry Ainley as Hassan, Leon Quartermaine as Ishak and Cathleen Nesbit as Yasmin. Eugene Goossens was the conductor of the orchestra. The Serenade from *Hassan* became very popular and did an immense service to Delius by introducing him to the public at large. He struggled over to London for late rehearsals and the première and Leon Quartermaine remembered over forty years later what a difficult job it was for them to get the wheel-chair down into the stalls, where Delius sat and commented. At one point in the dress rehearsal a scene change had not been effected in time for the curtain to go up when it should have done, and Goossens had no alternative but to repeat the interlude. Delius was aghast and called out in his rather thin voice: ' No,

Mr Goossens! No, no, no! Not again, you mustn't play it again!' It was then explained to him what had happened; it took him most of the rehearsal to get over the incident.

During the composition of *Hassan* it had been evident to Delius that he must dictate the work in order to finish it and he desperately sought for somebody to act as his assistant. Jelka was obliged to continue in this capacity but she was not quick enough and the effort exercised his patience so much that his health was not improved. In order for him to be able to give form to the other musical thoughts which he was carrying about with him, someone far better qualified was needed to act as scribe. Delius cautiously asked Philip Heseltine but he refused outright.

Toward the end of the year Delius bought a car—a Ford with yellow curtains in the back windows. It lived under the archway of the main gate of the house during the winter months and was a great boon to Delius and Jelka, enabling them to get out much more easily to the market in Moret once a week—an outing which he greatly enjoyed when he was feeling well enough. That autumn they went to Cannes to visit the Clews and spent Christmas in Rapallo.

The better weather in February 1924 encouraged Delius to begin composition of a violin sonata. Some electrical treatment which he had received in Cassel was painful but effective; however, the constant perambulation round the spas and *Kurhäuser* of Germany, together with the upkeep of male nurses, was costing the Deliuses a great deal more than they could afford. Fortunately funds were coming in fairly steadily and the bulk of frozen assets had been released, so had it not been for the heavy medical expenses there would have been no cause for them to worry.

During the winter of 1924 the *Mass of Life* was played in London, Vienna, Prague and Wiesbaden, which brought in an enviable sum in royalties; but France remained stubbornly anti-Delius despite the fact that it was virtually his own country. In November he returned to Cassel for another cure, which enabled his hands to regain their powers, and by Christmas he was able to write to Henry Clews himself, saying how well he felt. But the improvement was desperately short-lived. Early in 1925 a dreadful reaction set in, reversing all the good that had recently been achieved by the doctors. Delius became greatly enfeebled and by July had

completely lost his sight. Since he could no longer walk he spent most of
the day in the Grez garden, sitting in his wheel-chair with the sun on
him, being read to by a German male nurse. All the running of the
house was centred round him, every event was timed to suit his convenience and everything happened at exactly the same time every day.
Delius's mental acuteness and fiery spirit remained utterly at variance
with his flesh, zig-zagging ceaselessly inside that shell of a body which
seemed almost too fragile to contain such huge nervous energy.

Fortunately he was not forgotten by the outside world. He and Jelka
were often embarrassed by the number of people, executive musicians
included, who wanted to help and to cheer him. Many was the time that
instrumentalists had to be thanked and hustled away after only one
movement of a particularly hated composer. The serious turn which his
illness had taken now meant that it was practically impossible for him to
leave Grez and certainly neither he nor Jelka considered it. He was particularly sorry to miss the London performance of the *Mass of Life*, given
at a Royal Philharmonic Concert on 2nd April by Paul Klenau. The
work was continuing to be widely played and was heard five more times
in Germany between Christmas and May 1926.

In that month the Deliuses had a wireless set on trial, as the BBC's
new service in Savoy Hill was powerful enough for the signal to be
picked up in Grez. Adine O'Neill, who never liked playing the piano
in public, took to the new medium with gusto, for alone in the studio she
found she could play without nerves. Delius listened to her performances
of the Mozart piano sonatas over a number of evenings and found this a
tonic. By 1927 it was clear that whatever hopes there might have been for
his recovery had faded completely. He knew this too and withstood the
knowledge nobly, optimistically taking any new cure which was
offered. His patience and fortitude under the extremes of pain which he
suffered were marvellous; the stoic in him revealed itself not only in his
severe, Roman appearance but also in his behaviour. The end of 1927
saw the performances of the *Mass* in Berlin and of *A Village Romeo* in
Wiesbaden and very many individual performances of other compositions all over Germany.

In the spring of 1928 Percy Grainger married a Swedish girl of great
beauty called Ella Viola Ström, at an extraordinary ceremony in the

Hollywood Bowl. He brought his bride to Grez during their honey-
moon a few months later, when they talked to Delius, took him on the
river and brought him up to date with what was going on outside Grez.
He was little interested in English composers, avowing that none
existed and that 'Parry would have set the whole Bible to music if he had
lived long enough'. But he always liked to hear about his friends,
particularly those in London, and asked searching questions about them.

While he was undergoing another cure in Wiesbaden he received
from a young Yorkshireman called Eric Fenby a letter of sympathy,
which he answered personally. Thus encouraged, Fenby wrote again to
offer his services, especially in the taking down of music by dictation. He
had read of Delius's sad predicament and had been sincerely moved.
Jelka accepted Fenby's offer with alacrity. Delius had been particularly
interested in the fact that Fenby was self-taught, like himself, and therefore
not stuffed full of what he considered to be academic rubbish. Yet Fenby
possessed a real talent and also managed to withstand Delius's rough
treatment until they together evolved a *modus operandi*. At first Fenby was
unable to understand what Delius was trying to communicate, for the
composer was unable to pitch notes and everything was on a monotone.
Delius thought that Fenby was slow and dull, and the arrangement
looked like breaking down altogether until Jelka advised the bewildered
and miserable young man (he was twenty-two) to persevere and at all
costs to stick up for himself without fear of Delius—even to criticize what
Delius was suggesting if he was able to prove his point.

The book which Fenby has left as a permanent record of his time as
Delius's amanuensis is most interesting, particularly in his description of
the way in which Delius worked in this autumn of his composing life.
He might build a whole work on one bar of a forgotten composition; indeed, as Fenby says, 'the score of *A Village Romeo and Juliet* contains the
germs of all the music that was to come after it, and is a happy hunting
ground for people who have time for this sport'. Delius often felt the
need to dictate new ideas—ideas which had suddenly come to him at
unexpected moments—and then he called out each note in a chord,
perhaps a few notes of the melody in whatever instrument he thought of
it, mentally hearing the sounds of an orchestra but being totally unable,
except by this method, to indicate what he meant. Sometimes Fenby

FACSIMILE OF A PAGE OF AN UNPUBLISHED SONG
('That for which we longed')

played a fragment at a time to ensure that he had down what Delius wanted; sometimes he made suggestions. Delius was always exhausted after these sessions and there were times when he told Fenby to destroy their efforts of the previous day and start again.

Fenby also describes the visitors to Grez, in particular Grainger, whose energy was enormous, despite the fact that he ate very little (he was also a total abstainer from alcohol and tobacco). Then there were Evlyn and Grace Howard-Jones, pianist and violinist respectively, who lived in the village and came in to play to Delius. Balfour Gardiner was a fairly fre-quent guest, as were Beecham and Dora Labbette. A friend of standing and a great character was the international cellist Barjansky, for whom Bloch wrote *Schelomo*. He had played the solo part at the première of Delius's Cello Concerto in Vienna in 1921 and had met Delius through Percy Grainger. It has been said that Barjansky was so small that he was able to stand his cello case open and change his clothes inside it; yet his stature and his curious appearance were altogether forgotten when he played. His wife was a sculptress in tiny wax models of people; she made one of Delius's head. Her significantly detailed descriptions of Delius and of Jelka are revealing:

Delius was a ghost, emaciated, bloodless, his long body as stiff as a corpse. There was great spiritual beauty in his face, the forehead high and noble, the eyes unusually deep-set, the eyelids heavy and half closed, the nose thin and aquiline, the mouth fine and beautiful in shape. His narrow pale hands lay helpless on his knees. His gray hair was long, so long that it fell over the open collar of his white silk sport shirt, revealing his long thin neck with a large Adam's apple. He did not wear a necktie; his suit was of light Shantung; his shoes were white suède. Everything about his appearance betrayed the great and thoughtful care his wife had given it. And despite his helplessness, he looked extremely elegant. . . .

And of Jelka:

Mrs Delius was then about sixty, pretty and kind. Something radiant and happy seemed to emanate from her, and we instantly struck up a warm friendship that endured until her death.

The most striking thing about her appearance was her extreme fairness. Her skin was milk-white and baby-pink, her eyes a pale blue-green, her hair gold-blond. She looked much younger than her years, tall, large, very feminine. She did not dress in a modish way, but in a manner that suited her, long, full dresses in light pastel shades, nearly always yellow and pale green, with bracelets and necklaces of Indian pearls and jade. Her appearance was artistic, and she gave the impression of being extremely *soignée*.[1]

The principal compositions which Delius and Fenby together committed to paper were *A Song of Summer*, the *Irmelin Prelude* and *Songs of Farewell*, together with the *Idyll*. This latter piece for solo soprano, baritone and orchestra was salvaged from the long-forgotten and never performed opera of 1902, *Margot la Rouge*, and was set to Walt Whitman's poem 'Once I passed through a populous city'. It was first given by Sir Henry Wood at a Promenade Concert in 1933 with Dora Labbette and Roy Henderson.

On 1st January 1929 Delius was created a Companion of Honour in the New Year's Honours List. The British public asked who Delius was. The gentlemen of the press were just as vague and sent some of their colleagues to Grez to find out more about the composer, unknown to many of them, who had suddenly achieved eminence. Beecham, who had been Delius's main sponsor for the C.H., decided that this was the time to launch a Delius Festival in London and he accordingly took it upon himself to arrange it. As a further result of this honour Delius was later invited to become a Freeman of the City of Bradford, which he accepted providing he need not travel there for the ceremony. He was afforded the intense pleasure and amusement of welcoming the Lord Mayor and Town Clerk at Grez, unsuitably clad and somewhat ill at ease, to bestow this thoughtful but nevertheless useless gift upon their long departed son.

Philip Heseltine, who had now become Peter Warlock, was co-opted by Beecham into writing the programme notes for the festival, generally assisting and being responsible for public relations. Beecham was doing Heseltine a favour and a great service, moreover, for he was in a precarious mental state. However this kind of work suited him perfectly and he made an excellent job of it. Since he had recently been through an anti-Delius phase in his worship of van Dieren and his music this helped to bring him back among his earlier friends.

[1] Both these descriptions are from *Portraits with Backgrounds* by Catherine Barjansky (New York, 1947).

With some difficulty Delius was persuaded that he must go to London and appear in person, as well as give himself the undeniable pleasure of hearing so many of his works performed within a short space of time. This had never before been possible. He agreed and on 6th October set out from Grez with Jelka. They stopped twice to rest before reaching Boulogne, put up at Folkestone for the night and arrived at the Langham Hotel (opposite the BBC and Queen's Hall in Langham Place)[1] on 9th October. He was in a collapsed state but recovered in the three days before the first concert on 12th October.[2] He was in London for three weeks and had to be carried through a throng of cheering people across Langham Place to and from Queen's Hall after each concert. At last he was known and his music was loved in England. But it had taken a long time since he had declared to his sisters: 'Some day I'll make the name of Delius known all over the world.' And it was very nearly too late for him to share in his own success. After Delius no one deserved more praise for the whole enterprise than Beecham, who had himself achieved the culmination of his labours, which had begun in 1907 and even now did not end with the completely successful 1929 Delius Festival.

It was while Delius was in London that he was invited by the Royal National Institute for the Blind to visit them and to dedicate one of his works to them. He chose the *Air and Dance* for string orchestra which he had composed in 1915. This clears up any possibility that he made the dedication at the time of composition, or that he had any premonition during the First World War of his impending blindness. After the London festival was over and he was on his way back to France he sat on the deck of the cross-Channel steamer and, turning his sightless eyes in the direction of the South Downs, asked that his chair might be turned round to face them. It is said that his features took on a different look as he imagined the sight and that this last reconciliation with the land with which he had been at loggerheads was the reason for his wish to be buried there.

A new visitor to Grez in 1930 was a hypnotist called Erskine who was

[1] Queen's Hall was destroyed by enemy bombardment on the night 10th–11th May 1941. The Langham Hotel is now BBC property, housing the BBC Club and offices.
[2] See Appendix G, p. 164, for full programmes of the festival.

able to work wonders through his remarkable talents. He made Delius walk a few unsupported steps and also enabled him to see shadowy objects. Whether this was a desirable course to take seems doubtful; the improvement lasted a pathetically short time before Delius lapsed into his normal state of paralysis and pain, which seemed worse than before, since his hopes had been raised and then dashed again, for ever.

Immediately before Christmas Delius was shocked and deeply upset to hear that Heseltine had died in London under circumstances which suggested suicide. The dichotomy of character and personality of Heseltine-Warlock seems to have got the better of him, coupled with a mysterious, secret unhappiness that had been more and more evident to his friends.

In 1931 Sir Henry Wood gave *A Song of Summer* at a Promenade Concert and Delius heard it on his wireless. The instrument was now firmly installed, but for an important broadcast arrangements had to be made to persuade other people in the village to turn off their electrical equipment at the vital times so as to avoid interfering with the music.

When Eric Fenby returned that year he took down the *Fantastic Dance* and the *Irmelin Prelude*. Mention has already been made of the song *Irmelin Rose* and the opera *Irmelin*. The *Prelude* is a short concert piece of four minutes duration, in the same key as the prelude to the opera and beginning in exactly the same way. But its greater economy and shape have turned what was a somewhat indecisive curtain-raiser into a miniature of great beauty. It makes great use of a theme:

which is heard in the opera, as well as once in the loosely constructed Prelude to Act I. In the song *Irmelin Rose* (seven years later than the

opera *Irmelin*), after an unfamiliar though beautiful start we find ourselves in familiar territory:

Ex. 7

It will be seen that the name 'Irmelin' occurs musically always as a
descending major fourth in the song and in the opera, except once in the
opera, when she tells her own name—and it rises.

The next new work, *Songs of Farewell*, was first performed by the
London Symphony Orchestra and the Philharmonic Choir at Queen's
Hall in May 1932 under Malcolm Sargent. Delius was most anxious that
his instructions should be carried out scrupulously in performance.
Fenby attended rehearsals, reporting to Grez that the work had been a
huge success. Nobody could have asked for a more tireless or painstaking
assistant. The celebrated portrait painter James Gunn was installed in

Grez when Fenby got back, painting the picture which is usually taken as representing the true Delius. This is unfortunate, for although it is a good piece of craftsmanship and tallies exactly with Catherine Barjansky's description, it is little more than a representation of a corpse.

Cecil Gray, Arnold Bax and Edward Dent all came to see Delius. Dora Labbette came too and sang his songs to him. Dent's recent biography of Busoni, which refers to Delius at Busoni's house in Berlin, interested the inhabitants of Grez and recalled happier times with great clarity. During the early, cold months of 1933 Lionel Tertis arrived all the way from Paris in a taxi. He was convinced that Grez lay in the suburbs, rather than 64 km. outside Paris. Once he had thawed himself out, he played his own arrangement for viola of the new Violin Sonata and brought Delius up to date with the musical life of London. In the early summer of 1933 Norman O'Neill paid his last visit, followed in June by the unexpected person of Elgar, who brought with him as a present the recently issued Volume I of the Sibelius Gramophone Society and an album of Hugo Wolf's songs. In bringing music by Sibelius he perhaps unconsciously reunited the three composers who had had major works performed at the Birmingham Festival of 1912: Sibelius, Elgar and Delius. The two men had never been at ease, socially, before. Now they warmed to each other during this one afternoon together. Elgar was most solicitous of the invalid's strength, signalling to Jelka to ask whether he should go, whether he was not overdoing his visit. He left in order to return to Paris to meet his young and brilliant protégé Yehudi Menuhin, then aged fifteen, who was to give a per-formance of his Violin Concerto there.

In the late autumn of 1933, when the nights closed in early in the narrow Grez streets, Jelka was knocked down by a cyclist and was forced to retire to bed. Clare's daughter Margaret was able to help them for a short while, acting as her uncle's nurse and companion. Although Jelka was up and about again before long, she was never perfectly well from then on. This was the first of a series of events which led straight on to Delius's death in June. On 23rd February Elgar died and on 3rd March Norman O'Neill succumbed to a blood clot after a minor road accident. Delius was distressed to hear that Elgar had gone, and heartbroken to hear about his friend O'Neill, of whom it was said in an obituary that, while his musical style was original, 'if he had any affinity it was with his great friend Delius'.

Since January Delius had been put on a saltless diet and was not allowed to eat any meat or fish or to drink alcohol. In April shooting pains at five every evening continued throughout the night and left him weak and exhausted in the morning, after literally fighting his way through the dark hours. As a result he was put under mild sedation and was given *pyréthane* by the French doctor to ease the pain. This upset him so much that he was unable to retain any food at all and grew considerably weaker. Unless his mind was continually occupied by conversation or by being read to, he was unable to sustain the pain. Neither was he able to rest in any one position for long without being moved.

Now Jelka's turn came, after sleepless nights and exhausting days. A thorough inspection revealed that she had cancer. She was operated on in Fontainebleau with success. They sent for Fenby, who came at once and ministered most tenderly to Delius while Jelka was in hospital, scarcely getting two hours' sleep in twenty-four, so demanding was the invalid's pain, so insistent were his cries. On 6th June Delius appeared to be sinking into a coma and on the following day the doctor came to give him morphia every four hours. Whenever he recovered consciousness he was in the greatest agony and this situation continued until the night of 9th–10th June. Jelka was called to him from her own hospital bed, with her incision still unhealed, and they kissed each other for the last time. Delius lapsed into unconsciousness and died at a little after four in the morning. Fenby was with him and had to break the news to Jelka. He telegraphed to Beecham, who was unable to leave London, and Dora Labbette went to Grez instead, arriving on the following morning. She stayed with Jelka, in her room, until after the funeral. She endeavoured to distract Jelka's attention while the death-mask was being made and later when Delius was being put into his coffin. But Jelka knew what was going on and bore it all stoically. In fact the tension of the past, worst years seemed to have been lifted with his passing, and Dora Labbette found Jelka calmer, as if she felt relieved of the burden which for so long she had helped to bear.

Fenby has recounted in detail how he was given charge of the arrangements for Delius's pagan burial in Grez and how the body was exhumed from its temporary grave in May 1935 and taken to England. This was arranged by the Harrison sisters who came to Grez to see Jelka in the late summer of 1934 and persuaded her to agree to his final resting place being in Limpsfield, near their own mother's grave, so that they might always tend them both. It was unlikely that anybody in Grez was going to feel strongly enough about tending a pagan grave, and in any case Jelka knew that her own time was short. Catherine and Alexander Barjansky spent several weeks with her in Grez, but it was clear to them that the pale shadow of Delius's wife had nothing left to keep her on earth. During the last week of May, when Delius's body was being brought across the Channel, she went to England, was admitted to a Kensington nursing home and became seriously ill again. Consequently she was unable to attend the funeral at Limpsfield on Sunday, 26th May.

Beecham presided over the service at which a section of the London Philharmonic Orchestra (strings, woodwind and harp) played *Summer Night on the River*, the Serenade from *Hassan* and *On hearing the first Cuckoo in Spring*, and then he led the procession out of the church to the laurel-lined grave where he gave an oration. He said that Delius was a wanderer, almost an exile. He was born in the age of Carlyle, Matthew Arnold and Ruskin and strove to escape from the hard, arid business of northern England; and he did escape. The British war of idealism caused him to turn inquiringly to the shores of his native land. Beecham ended with these words: 'We are not here in a spirit of vain regret but rather one of rejoicing that his work is with us and will remain with us for evermore.' He sent Jelka some gramophone records of the service for her to hear afterwards but on the next day, 28th May, she died and was buried next to her husband in Limpsfield. She had survived Delius by less than a year. During that time she had worked to put at Beecham's disposal a great deal of information and material for his biography, but she too had been struggling against the inevitable. 'I shall never be my old self again,' she had said, 'but what does it matter now?'

CHAPTER VI

DELIUS'S CRAFT

THE PARTICULAR magic which makes Delius's music unlike any other, and the technique which he uses to express himself, has not often been explored. The current trend away from analysis may be one reason; the disinclination to dissect the butterfly may be another. For the clumsy hands that tear at delicate fabrics can never determine the origin of that colour or fragility, that special character and texture. Some people may feel that the music of Delius is so finely wrought, so delicate in its construction that a brisk cut of the dissecter's knife would make it fall to pieces, never to be reassembled. But this is far from so. In fact the very contrary seems to happen: the more one inspects a Delius score and examines its elements, the more closely it seems to be bound together— providing the elements are preserved intact.

Of the two main elements of composition—melody and harmony— Delius relies largely upon harmony to achieve his effect, while the relationship between his melody and harmony is very different from that of his contemporaries. He wrote comparatively few melodies of the kind that can be instantly reproduced and 'whistled by errand-boys' (an asset which he found distinctly distasteful because they were unlikely to be whistled in the correct rhythms or at the proper pitch). Nor did Delius employ counterpoint, especially as he found Bach, its greatest master, to be deadly dull. It is in harmony and orchestration, the skilful pointing of the right instruments to bring the only possible sound at any particular moment, that Delius instantly succeeds and makes his own music unique and unmistakable.

As Delius grew older, riper and at the same time more physically infirm, his style of composition changed. The works became shorter and shorter, the contents more charged with passion and urgency; yet the brevity of the musical form must be attributed not only to a new shape in

his thought but also to—and probably because of—the changed harmonies which he was building into these works, so concentrated that they
became their essence. The harmonies are original, entirely English in
idiom and in no way connected with any other school of composition.
Nor do they seem to have inspired the work of younger composers, apart
from a few transitory compositions by friends and admirers like Bax,
Bantock and Warlock. Delius fathered no legitimate children, neither
physical nor musical; yet he can claim a number of musical uncles even
if his parenthood in this respect is totally obscure.

Particularly in his early work, and possibly unconsciously, Delius
followed Wagner. The same may be said of Chopin's style; it is impossible to believe that Delius was not given something of this composer's advanced manner on that curious tour of Norway (see pp. 37–8).
Grieg most certainly inspired him, and it is in the added sixths and
ninths of both composers that they incline towards each other most
obviously. This excerpt from Grieg's *Ballade*, Op. 24 might almost have
been composed by Delius, were it not for the typically Norwegian E♮,
in the last bar which Delius would not have used:

Ex. 8

The other formidable influence on Delius was that of the anonymous folksong composers of the past. Firstly it was the Negro tunes which he heard in Florida, with the aroma of Africa still upon them, though fading as the generations passed. In this connection it is curious to think that Delius and MacDowell seized on this African music and used its flavours with great discretion before Gershwin took it and fashioned it in his way to found a whole new genre of folk music. And after Gershwin the jazz men extracted from it the wildness and even the brutality which matches the baser instincts.

We know that Delius found Negro music fascinating, not only because anything truly natural and unspoilt appealed to him but also because he found in it the utterances of a musical race which expressed itself very differently from any other, and most potently at the same time. Only once did Delius reflect the savageness of Negro music in his own compositions and that was at certain moments in his opera *Koanga*; other-wise it was the sad, reflective and elemental aspects which he took and combined with entirely different, national colours.

The last influence which Delius welcomed was that of English folk-song, mainly through the intervention of Grainger and his researches and collections. With all these diverse influences at work Delius might have produced the strangest hotch-potch of sound imaginable. On the contrary most of his scores are models of good organization, so that the finished material appears utterly spontaneous. The more straightforward and simple a composition appears on the page the more likelihood there is of patient thought and effort and skill behind it all. Those who wish to detract from Delius's achievements can be expected to declare that his music is 'precious', lacking vigour, and formless; but these strictures spring from a lack of true understanding of what he was doing. The works which come in for the most criticism are not always those in classical form like the concertos, but the tone-poems which, written in a unique manner, cannot be listened to as if they were by Liszt or Strauss. Delius's music requires a fine adjustment of the senses: it is music for the connoisseur.

When he was a young man he used to sit at the piano and play a chord which he fancied—a chord which he either invented or else extracted from somebody else's composition. He would then repeat the chord up

Ex. 9

and down the keyboard in isolation and in every key. Then he would enclose it in two different chords which either came to mind at once or were worked on until he was satisfied with them and again he would go up and down, now with the three chords, until he had exhausted all parallel harmonic possibilities. At this time in his life his two main sources were Chopin and Wagner: one the master of the piano, the other the master of the orchestra. They both gave Delius all he wanted as a basis for his own practical harmony at the keyboard. Throughout his life, while he possessed all his faculties, he composed at the piano.

Delius's harmonies both adhere to and break the stern rules which his professors at Leipzig tried to din into him. Many of these rules were anathema to him, and he did not let them influence his musical character. He boldly doubles fifths and octaves, he gives the chorus basses different lines from the orchestral bass (see Ex. 9, p. 96) but breaks the conven, tions in order to achieve an effect.

There seems to be one rule which he follows, since his mode of expression tends to be shaped so as to coincide with it. This is his bass line which very frequently descends gently, often chromatically, or alternatively one of the inner parts may make such a 'falling movement' (as I shall call it) while the bass remains static. Since the bass is the foundation of all harmony it is all the more important to notice this because Delius's chords seldom follow a classical progression. In the preceding quotation from *Sea-Drift* the bass line descends gently and settles finally (on second bassoon and contra bassoon) on the tonic E. The baritone melody is not very interesting in itself: it is the chorus that sup, plies the main interest which brings the ensemble to life. Yet even with these fairly early and modest Delian ideas, the example achieves the triple effect of being harmonically interesting, melodically interesting and characteristic of the composer.

Descent is a feature of Delius's composition, and it contributes largely to the poignant feeling inherent in the majority of his works. This is the 'falling movement' which also gives the atmosphere of despair, even tragedy, when subtle harmonies are pressed into service as well. This moment from *Appalachia* may help to illustrate the point (the orchestral accompaniment, apart from the bass, is omitted):

Ex. 10

The Nature pieces are given a strangely realistic slant by the use of this device, for everything in Nature eventually falls when it dies, except water, which falls as it lives. It may thus be possible to see in all this another view of Delius in his constant awareness of, or emphasis upon, Destiny and its implacable presence—a force which he tended to scoff at in early life but to lean towards as it approached him. The poems which he chose to set are infected with this small obsession and the falling movement is everywhere apparent.

Sometimes, to achieve a choppy effect, Delius does not write those inversions of chords which give a smooth bass line, but places his more-or-less unrelated chords cheek-by-jowl on the stave. The result of placing unusual bedfellows like this can produce a phrase as arresting as this one from the *Second Dance Rhapsody*, where the harp part gives us all we need to know:

Ex. 11

In such an apparently haphazard arrangement of chords one begins to wonder what happens to the inner parts in scored passages where there is this sort of progression. Surprisingly, they invariably remain interesting, sensible to play and vital. This is seen in the dilemma of the chorus-

master before a performance of *Sea-Drift* (see p. 57) which was brought about by his inability, at first, to understand that Delius's harmonies do not proceed 'normally'.

This does not mean that they proceed without any plan, though it may not be one which was understood at Leipzig. Generally speaking, Delius's music is not strictly tonal. There is always a definable harmonic centre, but it changes so rapidly that it is not possible to say that the key is this or that when we come to the more advanced compositions. In this respect there is a great deal of similarity with Debussy's harmonic methods, particularly in *Pelléas* which, he said, dispensed with 'any musical development of a parasitic nature'. Delius eschews normal development, and while he does not copy Debussy's style in any way, the general direction of the two composers was the same.

Delius's harmony depends on what are technically discords to achieve its effect. Apart from added sixths and ninths, he takes what to another composer would be an unresolved chord and makes it the basis for a 'take-off' to a different harmonic region, avoiding any resolutions even at the end of the piece, and thus giving the music its particular quality of remoteness. His music is not earth bound; it hovers. Ex. 12, p. 101, may help to clarify this statement (woodwind have been omitted). It comes from the *Requiem* (Fig. 4) and shows the 'sliding' harmony that never gives us the opportunity to come to rest in any specific key. Note also the horn part which carves its own way, seemingly irrespective of the baritone voice, and the time-signatures which, in changing, add to the feeling of being removed from reality, though never making us feel exactly insecure.

I shall later take two Delius tone-poems for analysis, but in passing I must mention another, *In a Summer Garden*, which is among the best examples of his art. There is an interesting dichotomy of opinion between two acknowledged Delians concerning the melody in this work. First Neville Cardus [1] considers:

. . . there are definite themes, even long-phrased melodies, and they are developed and diversified with a sure and happy touch; the melodiousness of *In a Summer Garden* is such, that for all its harmonic implications and its

---

[1] From *Ten Composers* (1945), chapter on Delius, p. 148.

GROUP OF ARTISTS
AT GREZ IN THE
MID 1870s

including

1 F. B. Chadwick

2 Emma Löwstädt

3 Jean-Baptiste Corot

4 Robert Louis Stevenson

5 Frank O'Meara

6 Middleton Jameson

Ex. 12

importance as texture, it can be sung or whistled throughout; even when the harmonies move and modulate without apparent regard for a tonal centre, the melodic contours are never seriously imperilled.

Cardus goes on to compare the connection between theme and orchestral tissue with the only two similar, purely orchestral compositions that exist: *L'Après-midi d'un faune* and the *Siegfried Idyll*. Contrary to this assessment, Heseltine [1] believed it no exaggeration to say that

apart from a flowing tune in the middle section there is not a single theme in the work; yet the effect of a continuous outpouring of melody is achieved by the subtle manner in which rhythm and melodic fragments are merged together into broad effects of light and colour that suggests the vivid luminous canvases of the gracious lady who inspired the work.

The *Oxford Companion to Music* defines melody as '. . . what catches the ear . . . the man in the street who demands that music must have melody before anything else is right in principle . . .'. We have to have something to grasp in an unfamiliar piece of music to give a clue to its main flavour; the melody is the easiest way to it. Delius did not write for the man in the street; for a long time he wrote for himself and scarcely, if ever, considered the large mass of potential listeners to his music. But there are a number of melodies in his compositions which contradict the statement that they were subservient to their harmonies: the tune in the *First Cuckoo*, the slave tune in *Appalachia* (the theme), the Serenade from *Hassan*, *La Calinda* from *Koanga* and so on. Of these the *First Cuckoo* theme comes from a Norwegian folk tune; [2] but, in spite of its apparent Norwegian flavour in the melodic line, the first *Dance Rhapsody* does not, and must be taken as original. The slave tune in *Appalachia* is a genuine Negro melody; the Calinda is also a Negro dance which Delius first used in the *Florida Suite* and which is probably as authentic as when he first heard it; and the Serenade from *Hassan*, though sounding redolent of folksong,

---

[1] Quoted by Edwin Evans, as Heseltine's words, in a Beecham concert programme note in 1951.

[2] Called in Norwegian *I Ola-Dalom* (In Ola Valley), No. 14 of Grieg's 'Nineteen Norwegian Folk Songs', Op. 66, for piano.

cannot be traced and must be taken as original. Apart from these outstanding melodies there is the theme upon which Delius built *Brigg Fair*, a folksong collected in Lincolnshire by Percy Grainger.

There is a parallel here between Delius and the dramatic poet Christopher Fry. Fry is able to write the most lovely words, clothed with exquisite choices of phrase and figures of speech, commanding the language with a brilliance and dexterity that for range of expression have probably not been equalled since Shakespeare. But he finds it difficult to invent a good plot upon which to rest his characters and cause them to interact. Delius likewise chooses and orchestrates his harmonies with great skill; they are far more interesting than his melodies. Nevertheless, now and again he does invent a melody, though we have to search to find it. Once we have located it, however, we have also found the answer to why Heseltine was given to writing so passionately about Delius's music.

Brigg Fair and the first *Dance Rhapsody* have one effect in common—and it is a musical effect—in that the solo violin section (Fig. 23) of the *Rhapsody* is similar in conception to the middle section (Fig. 15) of *Brigg Fair*. But in the *Rhapsody* the theme is kept to, the only difference being in tempo, in note values and in the tessitura of the solo, which is suddenly so different from what has gone before. Here is the theme expressed as a languid melody:

Ex. 13

However, this is an exception, and Delius's melodies, or rather his top lines, are by no means as ingratiating to the ear as in this example. Sometimes they are nothing more than melodic lines in the manner of recitative, especially when sung, like many examples to be found in *Sea-Drift*. In the composer's later life they appear, if taken away from the rest of the score, to have no connection with it, like the previous example. One can say that Delius's mature music is not written as a melody with harmony and orchestration but as a combination of sounds, made possible by whatever group of instruments he has at his disposal, so arranged as to portray to the best of his ability the sound-picture which he has in mind.

In this respect, one thinks of Wagner. By the time he had reached out to create *Parsifal* he was using the human voice as an extension of the instruments in the invisible Bayreuth pit and was, in consequence, still further freezing his drama. Delius was extending Wagner's discovery that each and every instrument, be it human or held by humans, was merely another colour in the musical texture and, in order to elaborate that texture to the full, must be used as such.

At a first hearing the melody may perhaps seem to be submerged, with recognizable shafts coming through; but very quickly it will be apparent that there is always melody waiting to be heard as it comes through the orchestral texture. For one who is steeped in the Delian way of music, Cardus must be believed when he says that he is able to whistle *In a Summer Garden* all the way through. It may be difficult, and it may not

bear another's hearing, but it is possible. Constant Lambert, who conducted Delius's music with great feeling and understanding, once said: 'It
is a sign of weakness in a composer's make-up when our attention is
inevitably directed towards one particular facet of his music—Delius's
harmony or Stravinsky's rhythm. . . .'[1] Sir Thomas Beecham contra-
dicted this in a broadcast talk on the opera *Irmelin* by declaring it to have
an abundance of melody. 'A good melody,' he asserted, 'is one which
penetrates the ear with facility and quits the memory with difficulty.'

It is almost as if Delius knew the secret of an advanced kind of melody
which he was unwilling to share with us; for as he approaches and
touches on the most profoundly beautiful melodic idea he will break off,
giving us a snatch, a whiff and no more. And when this happens as like
as not it will be with one of his own inventions. Eric Fenby puts it like
this: 'He alone among composers, or so it seems to me, gave us a glimpse
—no more—of the rapturous possibilities latent in soaring lyrical prose.'
And it is when it soars that Delius's melody is not only most effective but
also most characteristic. Nobody else seems to be able to get the same
kind of voice from a solo violin or cello or oboe or horn as he can. See, for
example, the tantalizing melody which occurs and reoccurs in the prelude
and postlude of the very unusual song *Cynara*, for solo baritone and
orchestra. There is a single chord here which is one of the most volup-
tuous that Delius ever wrote and the possibilities it offers for development
add to the disappointment that it only comes and goes, for ever. Development, as we know, was never Delius's way save in his different sets of
variations; but so far as harmonic development is concerned, he never
explored it.

Before going on to discuss Delius's use of instruments, it is better to
define his different periods of composition and to account for his development within them. These periods are as follows:

I   *Florida Suite* (1887) to *Paris* (1899).
II   *A Village Romeo and Juliet* (1900) to *Cynara* (1907).
III *Brigg Fair* (1907) to the Cello Concerto (1921).
IIIa Violin Sonata (1915) to the Cello Concerto (1921).
IV   The dictated, edited and arranged works of the latter years.

---

[1] Constant Lambert, *Music Ho!* (2nd ed., 1947).

The first period of composition contains many manuscript works that we cannot hear, so that at present *Florida* is the first, or rather the earliest composition in print. The three early orchestral pieces, *Summer Evening*, *Marche Caprice* and *Sleigh Ride*, have been edited, as has the opera *Irmelin*, but since it was Beecham's way to be entirely scrupulous with the original intentions, it is reasonable to assume that he merely added dynamics which were generally missing in Delius's MSS. Thus it may well be that (the early songs apart) it is the *Légende* for violin and orchestra [1] (in its reduction for violin and piano) which has retained the composer's original thoughts without any revisions. The edited version of the opera *Koanga* comes within this period and so do the first versions of both *Appalachia* and the Piano Concerto; but they are never heard in these earlier forms. *Paris*, which ends the first period, is published just as Delius composed it.

Questions may be asked about this editing. At the beginning of his composing life, the fifteen years which ended the nineteenth century, Delius was not only striving to express himself in a style which was as yet only half formed but he was also suffering from a limited technique because of his sparse and disjointed training. It is possible that these early works may later have been considered by the public at large to have been interfered with in a genuine desire to present them to the world in not so rough-hewn a manner. This is not the case. Reference to unpublished early editions now show that Delius always knew exactly what he wanted to say, but that he sometimes had second thoughts. At the same time he had little idea—nor did he care—about what the public wanted or expected; he hardly ever heard other composers' new works and was not at all abreast of musical developments around him. His musical voice was so unusual, even before World War I, that it needed to be put over in the most ingratiating manner possible.

Three songs begin the second period, but they give little indication of the immense sureness of the first major work in it, *A Village Romeo and Juliet*, indisputably his greatest opera. He then went on to compose the revised version of *Appalachia*, *Sea-Drift*, *A Mass of Life*, the single-

---

[1] Not, as the *Encyclopaedia Britannica* has for several editions stated, Delius's first published work. This was *Zum Carnival*.

movement version of the Piano Concerto, *Songs of Sunset* and *Cynara*, which at one time belonged to *Songs of Sunset*. If Delius had written no more after *Cynara* his name would have been assured, but he went on to extend and strengthen his style with *Brigg Fair*, in which his full voice was heard for the first time. This was the beginning of Delius's mature career, though there were times when his powers waned afterwards.

Overlaying this period III is another which I have called IIIa. It is the uneasy period which drew Delius into accepting classical moulds for his compositions: four sonatas, the Double Concerto, the Violin Concerto (ostensibly in one movement, but formally not), the String Quartet and the Cello Concerto. This concerto forms a satisfactory conjunction between III and IIIa. Thereafter he had to rely on assistance in notating his ideas, first of all from Jelka and then from Eric Fenby. The arrangements of works made with or without his knowledge and permission, which need not concern us here, and the last works of all—the desperate final outpourings of the crippled composer—take the final period up to 1932. With Fenby's assistance his brain was as alert, as explicit as ever, and the *Songs of Farewell* are a truly remarkable endeavour under the difficult circumstances which both Delius and Fenby were obliged to suffer.

Together with his eventual assurance as a unique harmonist Delius was always able to clothe his musical thoughts with unerring skill and assurance. His scores show a complete understanding of the feeling of the pieces and, while he may often (more often than not) employ very large forces, he never allows his orchestra to thicken so much that it distorts the true intention; nor if there are voices to accompany are they ever swamped. He had a great facility for balance and texture, which many others spent a lifetime trying to find.

Delius's lack of touch with the outside world may have been one of the reaons why he still clung to huge orchestras when so many of his composer-colleagues, all too aware of increasing costs of performances, were becoming economical in statement. The chart on pp. 108–9 will give an indication of Delius's far from modest instrumentation in a number of selected works, and the reader will appreciate that, in itself, it tends to dissuade concert promoters from giving these works as regular repertory pieces. It is also apparent that his ideas about string strength in his orchestra differ greatly from the commonplace. While he

Delius

	Paris	Appalachia	Sea Drift	A Mass of Life	Brigg Fair	Dance Rhapsody I	In a Summer Garden
	1899	1902	1903	1904-5	1907	1908	1908
Flutes (incl. piccolo)	3	3	3	3	3	3	3
Oboes	3	3	3	3	2	1	2
Cor Anglais	1	1	1	1	1	1	1
Bass Oboe	—	—	—	1	—	1	—
E♭ Clarinet	—	1	—	—	—	—	—
Clarinets	3	2	3	3	3	3	2
Bass Clarinet	1	1	1	1	1	1	1
Bassoons	3	3	3	3	3	3	3
Contrabassoon	1	1	1	1	1	—	—
Sarrusophone	—	—	—	—	—	1 or contrabassoon	—
Horns	6	6	6	6	6	6	4
Trumpets	3	3	3	4	3	3	2
Trombones	3	3	3	3	3	3	3
Tuba	1	1	1	1	1	1	1
Timpani (no. of players)	1	1	1	1	1	1	1
Percussion (no. of players)	4	3	1	3	3	2	2
Celesta	—	—	—	—	—	—	—
Harps	2	2	2	2	1 (or 2)	2	1 (or more)
Soprano Solo	—	—	—	1	—	—	—
Mezzo Solo	—	—	—	1	—	—	—
Tenor Solo	—	—	—	1	—	—	—
Baritone Solo	—	1	1	1	—	—	—
4-part Chorus	—	1	1	2	—	—	—
1st Violins	16	16	16	16	16	16*	16
2nd Violins	16	16	16	16	16	16*	16
Violas	12	12	12	12	12	12*	12
Cellos	12	12	12	12	12	12*	12
Double Basses	12	10	12	12	12	12*	12

* A 'piccola orchestra', numbering 8.8.6.4.4., is employed from time to time.

The Song of the High Hills	North Country Sketches	Requiem	Dance Rhapsody II	Violin Concerto	Eventyr	A Song before Sunrise
1911–12	1913–14	1914–16	1916	1916	1917	1918
3	2	3	2	2	3	2
2	2	2	2	1	2	1
1	1	1	1	1	1	—
—	—	1	—	—	—	—
—	—	—	—	—	—	—
3	2	3	2	2	3	2
1	—	1	—	—	1	—
3	2	3	2	2	3	2
—	—	—	—	—	—	—
1 (or contrabassoon)	—	1 (or contrabassoon)	—	—	1	—
6	4	6	4	4	4	2
3	2	3	2	2	3	—
3	3	3	3	3	3	—
1	1	1	1	1	1	—
3	1	1	1	1	1	1
1	2	3	2	—	3	—
1	—	1	1	—	1	—
2	2	1	1	1	2	—
—	—	1	—	—	—	—
—	—	—	—	—	—	—
—	—	—	—	—	—	—
—	—	1	—	—	—	—
1	—	2	—	—	*	—
16	16					
16	16					
12	—	not specified	—	—	—	—
12	—					
10	—					

* The two 'wild shouts' require 20 men's voices.

asks for 16.16.12.12.12, the normal today (with 16 firsts) is 16.14.12.10.
8, that is to say eight players fewer than his specification and four of them
missing at the bottom. Another idiosyncrasy is the French preference
for three tenor trombones instead of the usual two tenors and a bass.
Further peculiarities are the occasional use of a bass oboe and the choice
of sarrusophone instead of the contra bassoon.

He employs the solo violin as he might a high soprano; and in vocal
and choral compositions he sometimes uses a double chorus (the *Mass* and
Requiem are more obvious examples); when he writes for a vocal solo
quartet, it is always a baritone and never a bass at the bottom. Apart from
the early and unknown *Sakuntala* and the *Late Lark* of 1925, which are
both for tenor and orchestra, Delius wrote consistently for baritone when
a man's voice was needed (*Cynara, Idyll*—with soprano, *Appalachia, Sea-
Drift, Nachtlied Zarathustras, Songs of Sunset*—with mezzo-soprano,
Arabesk, and the *Requiem*—with soprano). Not only is the solo violin a
feature of Delius's orchestration. The solo oboe is another instrument
which seems to assume a new and altogether Delian character when put
into his hand. Apart from the significant Calinda theme, which it plays
both in the *Florida Suite* and in *Koanga*, its contribution to the cold
temperature in 'Winter Landscape' from *North Country Sketches* is
notable; its introduction of the first theme in *Paris*, still soft and very
feminine, is most significant; its first statement of the *Brigg Fair* theme is
demonstrated in Ex. 15, p. 113. Delius was a consummate craftsman in
orchestration, which came only from patient study, trial and error and the
gift of knowing when he was right. His orchestration is never vulgar,
never shows any indulgence in coarseness or stridency any more than his
compositions show a vestige of these traits. His very modest use of percussion instruments is the best indication of this, while his demands for
unusual instruments are made purely for the purpose of obtaining the
exact colour which he cannot get otherwise at a particular moment. A
precise restraint is the very keynote in all he does.

It will be evident from the foregoing that Delius adopted certain
conventional forms of composition, at least in name, but that he also
developed forms of his own. In brief, he composed these works:

6 operas and incidental music to *Folkeraadet* and *Hassan*
A Mass of Life and *Requiem*.

5 works for solo voices and orchestra.
1 declamation with orchestra.
4 works for solo voice(s), chorus and orchestra.
2 works for chorus and orchestra.
5 songs for unaccompanied chorus.
over 50 songs for voice and piano.
23 orchestral works.
4 instrumental concertos.
3 smaller works for solo instrument and orchestra.
9 chamber works.
12 or so pieces for piano solo.
1 piece for harpsichord solo.
(Reference to Appendix B, p. 136, will give full details.)

If one did not know the composer, his list of works would give little or no indication that he was anybody but a nineteenth- or early twentieth-century composer who knew his market and wrote what was expected of him. Every conventional kind of composition is included, with one notable exception: there is no symphony. This at once gives us a clue to the person concerned. If there is no symphony it is likely that he is a miniaturist at heart, since a symphony must have development and re-development (although admittedly this is also needed in concertos). Delius's larger orchestral compositions are no longer than one movement of a symphony and are cast either as tone-poems or as sets of variations.

The frequency of the human voice in this list seems to imply that Delius was a specialist in its employment. Certainly in the two largest choral works, the *Mass* and the *Requiem*, this is the case. In certain others, which I shall deal with later, it also applies. But there are two areas of vocal music in which Delius has not proved himself completely: in opera and in songs with piano accompaniment.

The operas are not fully appreciated, with the exception of *A Village Romeo and Juliet*. Sir Thomas Beecham, who could be relied on to support Delius more staunchly than anybody else, said that it is 'the most consistently musical stage piece of its kind written in the last sixty years'.[1] He was careful enough to qualify his statement with the words 'of its

---

[1] In a broadcast in 1953.

kind' because there are very few operas which can be set alongside it. The nearest is Delius's last opera, *Fennimore and Gerda*, which in any case Beecham did not like. The important point about *A Village Romeo and Juliet* is its construction. Instead of being in the conventional acts and scenes, it falls into a series of tableaux. This was unheard of at the time Delius composed it: one wonders whether Berg's *Wozzeck* and *Lulu* sprang indirectly from the same idea. *Irmelin, Koanga* and (so we are told) *The Magic Fountain* have nothing new to offer so far as their form is concerned; while the Cinderella of Delius's operas, *Margot la Rouge*, remains only as the source from which the *Idyll* was created.

A Village Romeo and Juliet, it has been said, contains the germs of every one of Delius's future ideas. With this opera he seems to have crystallized his thoughts about form—certainly about harmony and the relationship of melody to it—and the orchestration is masterly. But since it is a tone-poem in operatic form it presents too fragile a vehicle for the cruel stage. No production of it in England has ever succeeded. Perhaps it might triumph as a film but it would scarcely be good box-office. This is the paradox of the work: it certainly succeeds on paper, it almost succeeds in the flesh, but it is still too ethereal.

The tone-poem, in his own form and to his own formula, is the kind of composition which suits Delius best and we can choose from among some fourteen of them [1] to discover what he was able to accomplish. The work which follows *A Village Romeo and Juliet* in chronological order and which follows on Delius's own thread of development is *Brigg Fair*. It shows him to have become more assured, more daring and to have achieved something more significant than before. He has been able to condense his thoughts into a far smaller compass than before, particularly more so than in his previous set of variations, *Appalachia*. He has not this time used a chorus, although he has needed the resources of a larger orchestra, but he has exercised his imagination far more compactly. It is hard to believe that Delius's real miniatures could ever have been composed without the economy of thought which is first evident in *Brigg Fair*.

An introduction precedes the exposition of the theme, then come six variations, an important middle section, eleven more variations and the coda, which restates the theme and ends the work. *Brigg Fair* consists of a little over 400 bars and takes a little more than fifteen minutes to play. Its content bears close examination. In Delius's centenary year an exhibition of his manuscripts included his original thoughts on the opening of *Brigg Fair*. This was a turbulent affair, quite different from the final result. As we know it, *Brigg Fair* opens in a pastoral manner:

Ex. 14   *Slow - Pastoral*

This is a flute solo over sustained strings and is of great importance in the whole work. This was undoubtedly as significant a second thought as the one Delius had in connection with *A Village Romeo and Juliet* (see p. 47).

While the composition is continuous, several of the variations are con-nected by short bridge passages, while others touch in the same bar. The melody of the theme is in the Dorian mode,[1] but even with this possibility of harmonic interest as the scale stands Delius introduces, in the greatest profusion, the most remarkable harmonies of his own. The simplest of these is to the plain statement of the theme, which goes like this:

Ex. 15

---

[1] That is to say, almost the same as the minor scale—in G here—but with its last three notes, E♮, F♮ and G, going upwards.

This theme is repeated three more times and harmonized differently upon each occasion. Each of these re-statements counts as another variation, each one has more complex and thicker harmony and all four versions of the theme are played without a break. Here is the second phrase of the third variation:

Ex. 16

The fourth variation is a slight melodic distortion of the theme, played staccato by the woodwind, with a running figure by half the first and second violins, while the remainder of the strings play pizzicato. The fifth variation has the theme played by first and third horns under running flute and clarinet in octaves, while the strings provide a transparent harmony in which the violas' falling movement is noticeable. The sixth variation gives the theme to the trumpet, and the woodwind and harp busily carve out a counter-theme in which this familiar Delian device occurs:

Ex. 17

The strings maintain a lightly scored but different harmonic texture from the previous variation, while at the point where there was originally a pause sign there is now a timpani roll.

There follows a contrasting section, which is required to be played 'slow and very quietly', the strings with mutes. Though it is not strictly a variation, it is one in the freer, romantic sense, as Rachmaninov might have done it:

Ex. 18

So far Delius has not strayed very far from the melodic pattern of the theme: it is his tempi, his orchestration and, above all, his harmonic ingenuity which have all provided the great variety of expression and interest which have taken us so far. The middle section of *Brigg Fair* contains one of his most idyllic and luxurious tunes, given initially to the first violins over seconds, and cellos holding sustained chords with

lapping flutes and clarinets above them. The melody is first introduced by
the two-bar flute figure (Ex. 14, p. 113). More and more instruments join
to swell the orchestral sound, though very softly. A solo horn brings about
the decline of the song-like melody until it dies away *pppp* with isolated
woodwind flicks of semi-quavers.

The variations proper begin again with the seventh, the shortest of them
all, in which the clarinet pronounces its version of the theme supported
by other woodwind and horns; harp and double basses enter on the last
bar of this variation, repeating themselves in the next bar, which turns
out to be the first of variation eight. This repeated bar across variations
seven and eight introduces the tubular bells, followed by timpani and a
variant of Ex. 17, p. 115, on double basses and harps. Near replicas of
these two bars end the variation.

As *Brigg Fair* progresses we find that each variation becomes more
intertwined with the one on each side of it. The ninth variation begins
with a version of the main theme in slow time on the flutes, oboes and
clarinets, to which the first violins supply a counterpoint:

Ex. 19

Suddenly at the eighth bar of this variation, and for the first time, almost
the full orchestra sounds as the tempo and dynamics both increase. Lower
woodwind and strings are in contrary motion downwards to the upward-
moving horns. There is activity on the timpani and the melody is
sustained by flutes and oboes, very necessarily reinforced by trumpets and
the first trombone. Imperceptibly, and in the same bar as that in which

the ninth variation ends, the tenth takes over, and instead of the *Brigg Fair* melody, it is the first violins' counter-melody (Ex. 19, p. 116), now coming fully into its own and doubled by the clarinet. The full orchestra (without percussion) is unleashed in proclaiming this idea until, with a *diminuendo* and *rallentando*, it dissolves away quite suddenly and the bass clarinet leads us into the eleventh variation.

This is entirely different from any that have gone before. It is slow, solemn and very deliberate. Trumpets and trombone mark out a square-cut version of the *Brigg Fair* theme, with an off-beat accompaniment for strings and an intermittent note for tubular bells. The double basses join in half way through the third bar as part of the building-up process, although the melody here sounds as if it is disintegrating, and while drooping modulates upwards into G♯ Dorian, a semitone higher than the G Dorian in which we expect to find the theme. This, the twelfth variation, returns the *Brigg Fair* melody to its proper shape, but retains the syncopated accompaniment of its predecessor.

Another transition returns us to the flute motif (Ex. 14, p. 113) which we last heard at the beginning of the middle section. This time it might be considered a variation upon itself, with entirely different scoring of tremolo upper strings and A–C crotchets on timpani and cellos, with a pedal A on the lower woodwind and basses. The cor anglais has a short solo:

Ex. 20

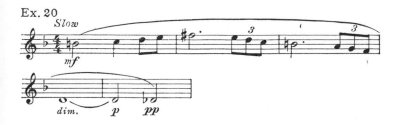

which contains the familiar triplet figure, now seen with the flute flourish (Ex. 14, p. 113), of all these transition passages. The thirteenth variation is in 3/8 time, marked 'Gaily'; it has a festive accompaniment to the original tune on the clarinet, with a counterpoint for flute above it, over

117

a pedal G on the third bassoon and a regular crotchet-quaver rhythm on timpani (also on G). The four horns play a kind of aside in quartet, in which the first produces a good example of the falling movement. The triangle is heard for the first time, one beat to the bar throughout the variation, while the flutes end with the now familiar falling triplets in a new guise and in extension, repeated and overlapping each other.

The fourteenth variation is given to the strings. Cellos declaim in Dorian D but with one intruding F♯ that should not belong to it. Above the melody the first desks of violins first of all cavort in arabesques for the initial phrase and then settle down to an exemplary piece of string writing, where the double basses reinforce cellos and everything moves downwards as if to gain strength for what is to come. The harp, which has been silent since the ninth variation, now opens the fifteenth. The tune is on clarinets and oboes and half the first violins. The variation closes in a *rallentando* that leads straight into a trumpet solo which begins the sixteenth variation.

This comes not at the beginning, but in the middle of the *Brigg Fair* theme, and gives way to a halting, almost stuttering four-bar version of it by the upper strings in unison. Now it leads into a 'straight' account of the melody, supported with most complex and diverse harmonies by nearly the full orchestra. They all come together in an *accelerando* transitional passage with familiar downward flourishes in quavers. The seventeenth and last variation is in a stately 3/2, proclaiming a kind of victorious ending with bass drum, tubular bells (in B♭, C and D), a sustained timpani roll on B♭ too, while trumpets blare out an unfamiliar version of the *Brigg Fair* melody. Trombones and tuba surprisingly play their version of the flute introduction (Ex. 14, p. 113). Gentler harmonies support a new idea of the former variation which is undoubtedly about to bring the work to an end. And as it becomes—as the direction in the score says—'softer and slower', the oboe cuts in as a preliminary to the coda and leads back into the *Brigg Fair* theme for the last time. Even now, Delius can provide a different harmony (see Ex. 21, p. 119), while the flute utters its little flourish for the last time. The work has ended, and in Delius's manner we are not perfectly sure exactly when: it goes out so very slowly that it fades, and in fading strains the ear for the last faint sound.

Ex. 21

Oboe

Strings &
horns

Brigg Fair contains not only the richest examples of Delius's harmonic invention but a great deal of his best orchestration, in which the potential of each instrument, as soloist and with a variety of others, is exploited to the full, showing that he possessed full command of the forces which he chose to have at his disposal. The work should contradict, by its very achievement, any criticism that Delius was not able to develop an idea. This is not symphonic development, because *Brigg Fair's* development of theme is in depth rather than in width, making more than one would have thought possible from the one simple melody. This economy, which Delius taught himself and which shows to great advantage here, was later put to use when he composed his miniatures for small orchestra : *On hearing the first Cuckoo*, the *Irmelin Prelude* and a possibly lesser-known work called *A Song before Sunrise*, which he dedicated to Heseltine. It shows Delius's art crystallized into the small space of 135 bars (six minutes' playing time) and written for a handful of instruments— double woodwind except for a single oboe, two horns and strings (divided except for the basses). It is in ternary form, with an extension (rather than development) of the idea in section *A* of thirty-four bars, followed by a centre section (*B*) of forty-five bars not far removed in content from its predecessor. This returns us to the identical thirty-four bars of *A* before an extended twenty-two bars of coda with which the work ends.

The *A* section is made up of the kind of melody which seems to invite counterpoint, canon or at least imitation. But Delius does not use these devices, though he goes as far towards imitation for the technique to include an occasional echo, but never for more than a bar or so. There are a number of prominent themes and figures in the work which we shall come to.

The first violins lead straight in without any form of preamble with an upward leap of a fifth at the beginning of the first theme. It lasts for a mere five bars before a flute figure, which is going to be very important, appears in the seventh bar, but not without its own easing-in process. In the fifth bar the flute distracts attention away from the violins, which are on a reiterated A, and doubles them as they move upwards, but then breaks away into a figure of its own (see Ex. 22, p. 121).

In the eighth bar the clarinet has this figure and in the ninth and tenth

Ex. 22

bars the violins take it up while the flute doubles them in the tenth bar.

Three times in the course of *A Song before Sunrise* there is a single bar of a different time-signature put in to adjust pace with shape. The first of these comes as the eleventh bar, and it is in 9/8 time, as against the 6/8 which has so far prevailed. Second violins and violas together illustrate the falling movement in the extra bar, and over into the next one (back in 6/8 again) as the tempo picks up and we hear a short, descending figure not unrelated rhythmically to the opening theme:

Ex. 23

1st Violins

It is a two-bar descent of a fifth, which is at once repeated, the second time reinforced by violas and the third time given out on the oboe in a modified form:

Ex. 24

It can only be the underlying harmony in the strings that gives to this little solo the indefinable certainty that, even in isolation, the two bars were written by Delius. A few bars later the music rises to a climax, with second violins, violas and cellos introducing a new version of the undulating rhythm:

Ex. 25

while the first violins play a variant of Ex. 22, p. 121, as a counterpoint.

Section B begins with the cellos stating Ex. 25 a tone lower, and then seven more bars follow to include a device for woodwind new to the work:

Ex. 26

Flutes

This brings us into an extra bar, this time in 3/4, played pizzicato by all the strings except the basses. The tempo slows and with Ex. 26 scampering about in the woodwind during the next five bars, we come to a 7/8 bar that brings a new atmosphere with it. This is helped (but scarcely audibly) by the second violins and violas playing on their bridges, a disembodied sound, after which the flute, then pairs of alternate lines of strings, play the same motif until we are brought almost to a halt. An arabesque on flutes and bassoons leads straight into a curious little section of six bars in 3/8. This puts us on a threshold, crossed in another three bars, and we are back in the familiar opening section again.

It takes us, identically, as far as letter I in the score. A longish coda is introduced by a strong and luscious figure on the violins. This asserts itself, but the rhythm of Ex. 26 returns to produce a whole new idea which Delius, as usual, casually dismisses among the riches of his invention. Instead of taking it any further, he leads us back into the theme that is so much associated with the cellos (Ex. 25). Immediately before this the flutes have introduced yet another figure which has not occurred before, made up of semiquavers in thirds that seem to come from the flute phrase in the last bar of the first section. The work fades its way out to silence on a string chord of C major with an added A in the violas.

Delius's Craft

While he respected a certain kind of law and order—a fact that his own meticulous scores underline—Delius was not solely a disciple of Nietzsche, with all that that implies. His music, which is his most secret utterance, shows him to be kind and gentle, though strong and forceful when necessary, but above all a believer in the 'All-Being', the omnipotent force of good which he asks us to worship with him as we hear it in everything he wrote.

APPENDIX A

(Figures in brackets in last column denote the age at which the person mentioned died; otherwise figures denote the age reached by the person by the end of the year concerned.)

Year	Age	Life	Contemporary Musicians
1862		Fritz Theodore Albert Delius born, Jan. 29, at Bradford, Yorkshire, son of Julius Delius, wool merchant.	Albéniz 2; Alkan 49; Arensky 1; Auber 80; Balakirev 25; Balfe 54; Berlioz 59; Berwald 66; Bizet 24; Boito 20; Borodin 29; Brahms 29; Bruch 24; Bruckner 38; Chabrier 21; Charpentier 2; Chausson 7; Cornelius 38; Cui 27; Dargomizhsky 49; Debussy born, Aug. 22; Delibes 26; Duparc 14; Dvořák 21; Elgar 5; Fauré 17; Fibich 12; Franck 40; Gade 45; Goetz 22; Goldmark 32; Gounod 44; Grieg 19; Halévy dies (63), March 17; Heller 49; Hiller 51; Hubay 4; Humperdinck 8; d'Indy 11; Ippolitov-Ivanov 3; Janáček 8; Jensen 25; Kirchner 39; Lalo 39; Lassen 32; Leoncavallo 4; Liadov 7; Liszt 51; Loeffler 1; Loewe 66; Lortzing 61; Lyapunov 3; MacDowell 1; Mackenzie 15; Mahler 2; Martucci 6; Massenet 20; Meyerbeer 71; Moniuszko 43; Mussorgsky 23; Offenbach 43;

Year	Age	Life	Contemporary Musicians
			Parry 14; Petrella 49; Ponchielli 28; Puccini 4; Raff 40; Reinecke 38; Rheinberger 23; Rimsky-Korsakov 18; Rossini 69; Rubenstein 33; Saint-Saëns 27; Serov 42; Sgambati 21; Sinding 6; Smetana 38; Stanford 10; Strauss (J. ii) 37; Sullivan 20; Svendsen 22; Taneiev 6; Tchaikovsky 22; Thomas (A.) 52; Verdi 49; Wagner 49; Wolf 2; Ysaÿe 4.
1863	1		Mascagni born, Dec. 7.
1864	2		d'Albert born, April 10; Meyerbeer (72) dies, May 2; Strauss (R.) born, June 11.
1865	3		Nielsen born, June 9; Glazunov born, Aug. 10; Sibelius born, Dec. 8.
1866	4		Busoni born, April 1; Satie born, May 17.
1867	5		Granados born, July 27.
1868	6	Violin lessons with Mr Bauerkeller of the Hallé Orchestra.	Bantock born, Aug. 7; Berwald (71) dies, April 3; Rossini (76) dies, Nov. 13.
1869	7	Violin lessons with Mr Haddock of Leeds.	Berlioz (65) dies, March 8; Dargomizhsky (55) dies, Jan. 17; Järnefelt born, Aug. 14; Pfitzner born, May 5; Roussel born, April 5.
1870	8		Balfe (62) dies, Oct. 20; Lekeu born, Jan. 20; Novák born, Dec. 5; Florent Schmitt born, Sept. 28.
1871	9	Goes to Preparatory School in Bradford.	Auber (89) dies, May 12; Serov (51) dies, Feb. 1.
1872	10	Hears Chopin's E mi. Waltz (Op. posth.).	Alfvén born, May 1; Moniuszko (53) dies, June 4;

Appendix A—Calendar

Year	Age	Life	Contemporary Musicians
			Skriabin born, Jan. 6; Vaughan Williams born, Oct. 12.
1873	11		Rachmaninov born, April 1; Reger born, March 19; Roger-Ducasse born, April 18; Séverac born, July 20.
1874	12	Goes to Bradford Grammar School.	Cornelius (49) dies, Oct. 26; Holst born, Sept. 21; Ives born, Oct. 20; Franz Schmidt born, Dec. 22; Schönberg born, Sept. 13; Suk born, Jan. 4.
1875	13	Hears *Lohengrin* at Covent Garden.	Bizet (36) dies, June 3; Coleridge-Taylor born, Aug. 15; Glière born, Jan. 11; Hahn born, Aug. 9; Montemezzi born, Aug. 4; Ravel born, March 7.
1876	14		Brian (H.) born, Jan. 29; Falla born, Nov. 23; Goetz (35) dies, Dec. 3; Ruggles born, March 11; Wolf-Ferrari born, Jan. 12.
1877	15		Dohnányi born, July 27; Karg-Elert born, Nov. 21.
1878	16	Removed from Bradford Grammar School and sent to Isleworth.	Palmgren born, Feb. 16; Schreker born, March 23.
1879	17		Bridge born, Feb. 26; Ireland born, Aug. 13; Respighi born, July 9; Jensen (42) dies, Jan. 23; C. Scott born, Sept. 27.
1880	18	Determined to become a musician. Joins the family business.	Bloch born, July 24; Medtner born, Jan. 5; Offenbach (61) dies, Oct. 5; Pizzetti born, Sept. 20.
1881	19	Goes to Stroud, Glos., as representative of the firm. Then to Chemnitz.	Bartók born, March 25; Enesco born, Aug. 19; Miaskovsky born, April 20; Mussorgsky (42) dies, March 28.

127

Delius

Year	Age	Life	Contemporary Musicians
1882	20	Studies violin under Hans Sitt in Chemnitz. Recalled to Bradford. Sent to Sweden (June 1). Travels to Norway. Is again recalled. Goes to St Étienne, gambles in Monte Carlo. To Paris and back to Bradford.	Grainger born, July 8; Kodály born, Dec. 16; Malipiero born, March 18; Marx born, Nov. 12; Raff (60) dies, June 24–5; Stravinsky born, June 17; Szymanowski born, Oct. 6; Zandanai born, May 28.
1883	21	Goes to Norway again and meets Ibsen.	Bax born, Nov. 8; Casella born, July 25; Wagner (69) dies, Feb. 13; Webern born, Dec. 3.
1884	22	Recalled to Bradford. Sails to Florida in March. Meets Ward. Undergoes 'crash' course of musical study with Ward until Sept.	van Dieren born, Dec. 27; Smetana (60) dies, May 12.
1885	23	Goes to Jacksonville (March), thence to Danville as Professor of Music at Roanoke College.	Berg born, Feb. 9; Hiller (73) dies, May 10; Riegger born, April 29; Varèse born, Dec. 22; Wellesz born, Oct. 21.
1886	24	Leaves Danville in spring. Goes to New York and disappears. Returns to Bradford in June en route for Leipzig Conservatorium.	Kaminski born, July 4; Liszt (74) dies, July 31; Ponchielli (51) dies, Jan. 17.
1887	25	Attends fewer classes and more concerts and opera. Goes for Norwegian holiday and meets Grieg and Sinding. Christmas party with them. Composes some songs and *Florida* suite.	Borodin (53) dies, Feb. 28; Toch born, Dec. 7; Villa-Lobos born, March 5.
1888	26	*Florida* suite performed in Leipzig to audience of two. D. leaves there at Easter. Grieg, in London, persuades D.'s father not to send him back to America. D. goes to France, lives in Ville d'Avray.	Alkan (74) dies, March 29; Heller (74) dies, Jan. 14.
1889	27	Composing mainly songs. Moves to Croissy-sur-Seine.	Shaporin born, Nov. 8.

Year	Age	Life	Contemporary Musicians
1890	28	Composes *Paa Vidderne* and commences *Irmelin* (opera). Frequent visitor to Mère Charlotte's.	Franck (67) dies, Nov. 8; Gade (73) dies, Dec. 21; Ibert born, Aug. 15; Frank Martin born, Sept. 15; Martinů born, Dec. 8.
1891	29	*Paa Vidderne* performed in Christiania. Song cycle *Maud*; continues *Irmelin*; Three English Love Songs. Meets Gauguin. Moves to Rue Ducoüédic.	Bliss born, Aug. 2; Delibes (54) dies, Jan. 16; Prokofiev born, April 23.
1892	30	Finishes *Irmelin*, composes (1st) Violin Sonata.	Honegger born, March 10; Kilpinen born, Feb. 4; Lalo (69) dies, April 22; Milhaud born, Sept. 4.
1893	31	Composes String Quartet. *Paa Vidderne (Sur les Cimes)* performed in Monte Carlo.	Goossens born, May 26; Gounod (75) dies, Oct. 18; Hába born, June 21; Tchaikovsky (53) dies, Nov. 6.
1894	32	Quarrels with his uncle Theodore. *The Magic Fountain* commenced.	Chabrier (53) dies, Sept. 13; Heseltine born, Oct. 30; Lekeu (23) dies, Jan. 21; Moeran born, Dec. 31; Pijper born, Sept. 8; Piston born, Jan. 20. Rubenstein (64) dies, Nov. 20,
1895	33	Composes *Over the Hills and Far Away*, two songs to poems by Verlaine, and *Légende* for violin.	Castelnuovo - Tedesco born, April 3; Hindemith born, Nov. 16.
1896	34	Meets Jelka Rosen for first time. They become close friends. Starts work on *Koanga*. Composes 1st version of *Appalachia*. Returns, briefly, to Florida.	Bruckner (72) dies, Oct. 11; Sessions born, Dec. 28; A. Thomas (84) dies, Feb. 12.
1897	35	Prolific year for composition: finishes *Koanga*, sets Seven Danish Songs, 1st version of Piano Concerto and incidental music for *Folkeraadet*. Conducts	Brahms (63) dies, April 3; Cowell born, March 11; Korngold (E. W.) born, May 29.

Delius

		Folkeraadet in Christiania and meets Ibsen for last time. Jelka buys the Grez house and D. moves in.	
1898	36	Death of Theodore Delius. D. buys Gauguin's *Nevermore*. Composes *La Ronde se déroule*, *Nachtlied Zarathustras* and Five Songs.	Harris (R.) born, Feb. 12; Rieti born, Jan. 28.
1899	37	In Yorkshire with sister Clare Black. To London for concert at St James's Hall on May 30. Composes *Paris*.	Chausson (44) dies, June 10; Chávez born, June 13; Poulenc born, Jan. 7; Strauss (J. ii) (73), dies, June 3.
1900	38	Composes two songs and starts work on *A Village Romeo and Juliet* (opera). Financially embarrassed.	Copland born, Nov. 14; Fibich (49) dies, Oct. 15; Křenek born, Aug. 23; Sullivan (58) dies, Nov. 22.
1901	39	Sells most of Florida plantation. *Paris* performed in Elberfeld. D.'s father dies. D.'s health first shows signs of deterioration.	Rheinberger (62) dies, Nov. 25; Rubbra born, May 23; Verdi (87) dies, Jan. 27.
1902	40	Composes competition opera *Margot la Rouge*; rewrites *Appalachia*.	Walton born, March 29.
1903	41	Composes *Sea-Drift*; marries Jelka Rosen, Sept. 28.	Berkeley born, May 12; Blacher born, Jan 3; Kirchner (79) dies, Sept. 18; Wolf (42) dies, Feb. 22.
1904	42	*Koanga* performed in Elberfeld, also *Appalachia*, Piano Concerto (1st version). Meets Cassirer.	Dallapiccola born, Feb. 3; Dvořák (62) dies, May 1; Kabalevsky born, Dec. 30; Petrassi born, July 16.
1905	43	Finishes composition of *Mass of Life*.	Lambert born, Aug. 23; Rawsthorne born, May 2; Seiber born, May 4; Tippett born, Jan. 2; Dag Wirén born, Oct. 15.
1906	44	Recasts Piano Concerto in one movement. *Sea-Drift* performed	Arensky (44) dies, Feb. 25; Shostakovitch born, Sept. 25.

Year	Age	Life	Contemporary Musicians
		in Essen. Finds a publisher. Sees Grieg for last time during summer holiday in Norway. At work on *Songs of Sunset* and *Cynara*.	
1907	45	*A Village Romeo and Juliet* performed in Berlin on Feb. 21. D. goes to London, meets the O'Neills and Beecham. Piano Concerto performed at Promenade Concert under Wood. Composes *Brigg Fair*. Close association with Percy Grainger. *Appalachia* performed in London and Beecham converted to D.'s music.	Grieg (63) dies, Sept. 4.
1908	46	D. conducts *Appalachia* in Hanley; commences composition of opera *Fennimore and Gerda*; composes *In a Summer Garden* and *Songs of Sunset*. Part II of *Mass of Life* performed in Munich. *In a Summer Garden* performed under D. in London.	MacDowell (46) dies, Jan. 23; Messiaen born, Dec. 10; Rimsky-Korsakov (64) dies, June 21.
1909	47	1st *Dance Rhapsody* performed under D. in Hereford. Complete *Mass of Life* given in London, then Elberfeld.	Albéniz (48) dies, May 18; Martucci (53) dies, June 1.
1910	48	D.'s health deteriorates. *A Village Romeo* given at Covent Garden; *Fennimore and Gerda* completed; friendship with Heseltine started. Meets Bartók.	Balakirev (73) dies, May 29; Barber born, March 9; Reinecke (85) dies, March 10; William Schuman born, Aug. 4.
1911	49	Goes for cure to Wiesbaden. Composes *Arabesk, Summer Night on the River*; commences *Song of the High Hills*.	Mahler (50) dies, May 18; Menotti born, July 7; Svendsen (70) dies, June 14.
1912	50	*Sea-Drift* given at Birmingham	Coleridge-Taylor (37) dies,

Year	Age	Life	Contemporary Musicians
		Festival—D. there. Sees his mother for the last time. Summer in Italy, meets Henry Clews. *First Cuckoo in Spring*.	Sept. 1; Massenet (70) dies, Aug. 13.
1913	51	Correspondence with Heseltine at its peak. Composes *I-Brasil* and starts *North Country Sketches*.	Britten born, Nov. 22.
1914	52	D. in London for first performances of *First Cuckoo* and *Summer Night on the River*. Returns to Grez in July but flees German advance at end of August. Returns after a week. German performances at an end. Composes Sonata for violin and piano (begun in 1905).	Liadov (59) dies, Aug. 28; Sgambati (73) dies, Dec. 14.
1915	53	Violin Sonata performed in Manchester. Composes *Air and Dance* for string orchestra, which is given privately in London, where D. stays with Henry Wood.	Goldmark (84) dies, Jan. 2; Skriabin (43) dies, April 27; Taneiev (58) dies, June 19.
1916	54	Completes *Requiem*, Violin Concerto, Double Concerto. Returns temporarily to Grez. Composing *Eventyr*; revises parts of *Arabesk*. Composes Cello Sonata.	Granados (48) dies, March 24; Reger (43) dies, May 11.
1917	55	Returns to England until end of the war. Financially pressed. Composes two Unaccompanied Choruses.	
1918	56	Composes *A Song Before Sunrise* and starts *A Poem of Life and Love*. Cello Sonata performed in London. Goes to Biarritz for a cure. Grez house sullied.	Boito (76) dies, June 10; Cui (83) dies, March 24; Debussy (55) dies, March 26; Parry (70) dies, Oct. 7.

Appendix A—Calendar

Year	Age	Life	Contemporary Musicians
1919	57	Performances in London of Violin Concerto, String Quartet, *Eventyr. Fennimore and Gerda* performed in Frankfurt and D.'s music re-established in Germany.	Leoncavallo (61) dies, Aug. 9.
1920	58	*Song of the High Hills*, Double Concerto and *A Village Romeo and Juliet* given in London. Accepts commission for incidental music to *Hassan*.	Bruch (82) dies, Oct. 2; Fricker born, Sept. 5.
1921	59	Composes Cello Concerto, given in Vienna by Barjansky (soloist).	Humperdinck (67) dies, Sept. 27; Saint-Saëns (86) dies, Dec. 16; Séverac (48) dies, March 24.
1922	60	Albert Coates gives first performance of *Requiem* in London. D. loses use of both hands. Summer in Norway.	Lukas Foss born, Aug. 15.
1923	61	*Hassan* performed in Darmstadt, then London. D. buys a motor-car. Autumn holiday in Cannes and Christmas at Rapallo.	
1924	62	Cure in Cassel; begins Violin Sonata; finances easier. Many performances of *Mass of Life*.	Busoni (58) dies, July 27; Fauré (79) dies, Nov. 4; Puccini (65) dies, Nov. 29; Stanford (71) dies, March 29.
1925	63	Greatly frustrated by inability to set down his thoughts. Jelka's efforts unsatisfactory. *A Late Lark* sketched.	Boulez born, March 25; Satie (59) dies, July 1.
1926	64	Enjoys the radio. Health very poor.	Henze born, July 1.
1927	65	No hope left for D.'s recovery. Many compositions performed all over Europe.	

Delius

Year	Age	Life	Contemporary Musicians
1928	66	Fenby arrives and becomes D.'s amanuensis.	Stockhausen born, Aug. 22; Janáček (74) dies, Aug. 12.
1929	67	D. created a C.H. Beecham organizes a D. Festival to which D. goes, arriving in London in October.	
1930	68	Fenby takes down for D. a number of compositions.	Heseltine (36) dies, Dec. 17.
1931	69		d'Indy (80) dies, Dec. 2; Nielsen (66) dies, Oct. 2; Ysaÿe (72) dies, March 12.
1932	70	D. given the Freedom of the City of Bradford. James Gunn paints D. at Grez. D. receives many distinguished visitors.	d'Albert (67) dies, March 3.
1933	71	Elgar visits D., as do Lionel Tertis and O'Neill. Wood gives the *Idyll* at Promenade Concert.	Duparc (85) dies, Feb. 13; Karg-Elert (55) dies, April 9.
1934	72	Jelka operated on for cancer. Fenby recalled and nurses D. until his death on June 10.	Elgar (76), dies Feb. 23; Schreker (55) dies, March 21. Alfvén 62; Auric 35; Bantock 66; Barber 24; Bartók 53; Berg 49; Berkeley 31; Blacher 31; Bliss 43; Bloch 54; Boulez 9; Brian (H.) 58; Britten 21; Chávez 35; Copland 34; Cowell 37; Dallapiccola 30; Dohnányi 57; Dukas 69; Falla 58; Glazunov 69; Goossens 41; Hába 41; Harris (R.) 36; Henze 8; Hindemith 39; Ibert 44; Ireland 55; Järnefelt 65; Kabalevsky 30; Kodály 52; Křenek 34; Lambert 29; Loeffler 73; Malipiero 52; Martin (F.) 44; Martinů 44; Marx 52; Menotti 13; Messiaen 26; Milhaud 42; Novák 64;

Year   Age   Life   *Contemporary Musicians*

Petrassi 30; Pfitzner 65; Pijper
40; Piston 40; Pizzetti 54;
Poulenc 35; Rachmaninov 61;
Ravel 59; Rawsthorne 29;
Respighi 55; Riegger 49;
Roussel 65; Rubbra 33;
Ruggles 58; Schmidt (F.) 60;
Schmitt 64; Schuman (W.)
24; Seiber 29; Sessions 38;
Shaporin 45; Shostakovitch
28; Sibelius 69; Sinding 78;
Stockhausen 6; Strauss (R.)
70; Stravinsky 52; Suk 60;
Szymanowski 51; Tippett 29;
van Dieren 50; Varèse 49;
Vaughan Williams 62; Villa-
Lobos 47; Walton 32; Webern
51; Wellesz 49; Wirén 29.

APPENDIX B

(This list has been specially prepared for the present work by Robert Threlfall, Assistant Archivist to the Delius Trust.)

COMPOSITIONS are listed under the following classifications:

Vocal Works:

- (*a*) Works for the stage
- (*b*) Solo voice(s) with orchestra but no chorus
- (*c*) Solo voices, chorus and orchestra
- (*d*) Chorus and orchestra
- (*e*) Unaccompanied chorus
- (*f*) Songs with piano accompaniment

Instrumental:

- (*a*) Works for orchestra
- (*b*) Solo instrument(s) and orchestra
- (*c*) Chamber music
- (*d*) Piano solo, etc.
- (*e*) Miscellaneous

Note: Delius usually dated his manuscripts; and likewise dates usually appear on published editions. In cases of works later revised, the dates may be those of the original version. In the following list, the dates have been taken from those manuscripts it has been possible to consult, or from the printed editions supplemented by information given in previous lists. Unpublished works are marked with an asterisk (*).

VOCAL WORKS

(*a*) Works for the Stage

Zanoni Opera (sketches)	1888
Irmelin Opera in three acts. Libretto by Delius	1890–2

Appendix B—Catalogue of Works

The Magic Fountain (*Der Wunderborn*)   Opera in three acts. Libretto by
    Delius   1894–5

Koanga   Opera in three acts with prologue and epilogue. Libretto by
    C. F. Keary   1895–7

Folkeraadet   Incidental music to the play by Gunnar Heiberg   1897

A Village Romeo and Juliet   Music drama in six scenes after Gottfried
    Keller   1900–1

Margot la Rouge   Lyric drama in one act. Libretto by Rosenval
    (Vocal score by Maurice Ravel)   1902

Fennimore and Gerda   Two episodes from the life of Niels Lyhne in
    eleven pictures. Libretto after J. P. Jacobsen   1909–10

Hassan   Incidental music to the play by James Elroy Flecker   1920–3

(*b*) Solo voice(s) with orchestra (no chorus)

Paa Vidderne (Ibscn)   Melodrama. Recitation with orchestral accom-
    paniment   1888

Sakuntala (Drachmann)   Tenor and orchestra   1889

Maud (Tennyson)   Song cycle for tenor and orchestra: 1891
                    Birds in the high hall garden
                    I was walking a mile
                    Go not happy day
                    Rivulet crossing my ground
                    Come into the garden, Maud

Seven Danish Songs with orchestra (see under (*f*) p. 138)   1897

Cynara (Dowson)   Baritone and orchestra   1907; finished 1929

A Late Lark (Henley)   Tenor and orchestra   1924–9

Idyll (Whitman)   Soprano, baritone and orchestra   1932

(*c*) Solo voices, chorus and orchestra

Mitternachtslied Zarathustras (Nietzsche)   Baritone solo, male chorus and
    orchestra (later included in *A Mass of Life*)   1898

Appalachia   Variations on an old slave song, with final chorus.
    Baritone solo, chorus and orchestra   1902

Sea-Drift (Whitman)   Baritone solo, chorus and orchestra   1903

A Mass of Life (Nietzsche-Cassirer)   Four soli, double chorus and
    orchestra   1904–5

Songs of Sunset (Dowson)   Mezzo-soprano, baritone, chorus and
    orchestra   1906–7

An Arabesk (Jacobsen)   Baritone solo, chorus and orchestra   1911

Requiem (Delius)   Soprano, baritone, double chorus and orchestra 1914(–16)

Delius

(d) Chorus and orchestra
The Song of the High Hills (wordless)   1911
Songs of Farewell (Whitman)   Double chorus   1930

(e) Unaccompanied chorus
Six part-songs with German texts   1887 and earlier
On Craig Ddu (Symons)   1907
Midsummer Song (wordless)   1908
Wanderer's Song (Symons) (male voices)   1908
Two Songs to be sung of a summer night on the water (wordless) 1917
The Splendour falls (Tennyson)   1923

(f) Songs with piano accompaniment
*When other lips shall speak   1880?
*Over the Mountains High (Bjørnson)   1885
*Zwei bräune Augen (H. C. Andersen)   1885
*Der Fichtenbaum (Heine)   1886
*Five Songs from the Norwegian: 1888
        Slumber Song (Bjørnson)
        The Nightingale (Welhaven)
        Summer Eve (Paulsen)
        Longing (Kjerulf)
        Sunset (Munck)
*Hochgebirgsleben (Ibsen)   1888
*Traum Rosen (Marie Heinitz)   1888
*Plus vite, mon cheval (E. Geibel)   1888
*Chanson [de] Fortunio (de Musset)   1889
*Seven Songs from the Norwegian: 1889–90
        Cradle Song (Ibsen)
        The Homeward Journey (Vinje)
        Evening Voices (Bjørnson) (orch. 1908)
          (also entitled 'The Princess' or 'Twilight
          Fancies')
        Sweet Venevil (Bjørnson)
        The Minstrel (Ibsen)
        Love concealed (Bjørnson)
        The Bird's Story (Ibsen) (orch. 1908)
*Four Songs to words by Heine: 1890–1
        Hör' ich das Liedchen klingen
        Mit deinen blauen Augen

Ein schöner Stern geht auf in meiner Nacht
Aus deinen Augen fliessen meine Lieder

Jeg havde en nyskaaren Seljefløjte (Vilhelm Krag)	1891?
Skogen gir susende langsam besked (Bjørnson)	1891
Three English songs (Shelley):	1891

    Indian Love Song
    Love's Philosophy
    To the Queen of my Heart

Lyse Naetter (On Shore how still) (Drachmann)	1891
Nuages (Richepin)	1893
Two songs to words by Verlaine: (later orchestrated)	1895

    Il pleure dans mon cœur
    Le ciel est pardessus le toit

Seven Danish songs: (originally with orchestral accompaniment)   1897
    *Summer Nights (On the Sea-shore) (Drachmann)
    *Thro' long, long years (also known as 'Red Roses' and
      'That for which we longed') (Jacobsen)
    *Wine Roses (Jacobsen)
    Let Springtime come (Jacobsen)
    Irmelin Rose (Jacobsen)
    In the Seraglio Garden (Jacobsen)
    Silken Shoes (Jacobsen)

Vier Lieder nach Gedichten von Friedrich Nietzsche: 1898
    Nach neuen Meeren
    Der Wanderer
    Der Einsame
    Der Wanderer und sein Schatten

Im Glück wir lachend gingen (Drachmann)	1898
The Violet (Holstein) (orchestrated in 1908)	1900
Autumn (Jacobsen)	1900
The Page sat in the lofty Tower (Jacobsen)	1900?
Black Roses (Josefson)	1901
Jeg hører i Natten (Drachmann)	1901
Summer Landscape (Drachmann) (orchestrated in 1903)	1902
The Nightingale has a Lyre of Gold (Henley)	1910
La Lune blanche (Verlaine) (later orchestrated)	1910
Chanson d'Automne (Verlaine)	1911
I-Brasil (F. Macleod)	1913

Two songs for children: 1913
    What does little birdie say? (Tennyson)
    The streamlet's slumber song
Four Old English Lyrics: 1915–16
    It was a lover and his lass (Shakespeare)
    So sweet is she (Ben Jonson)
    Spring, the sweet spring (Nashe)
    To Daffodils (Herrick)
Avant que tu ne t'en ailles (Verlaine)   1919

INSTRUMENTAL WORKS

(a) Works for orchestra
Florida Suite: Daybreak   1887
           By the River   (rev. 1889)
           Sunset
           At Night
Two pieces for orchestra: 1887–8
    *Sleigh Ride (see also Three Small Tone Poems)
    Marche Caprice (see also Petite Suite)
*Hiawatha   Tone Poem   1888
*Rhapsodic Variations (unfinished)   1888
Petite Suite d'Orchestre: 1889–90
    Marche (revised version of Marche Caprice)
    *La Quadroöne (Rhapsodie Floridienne)
    *Berceuse
    *Scherzo
    *Thème et Variations
*Idylle de Printemps   1889
*Suite for small Orchestra (in three movements)   1890
Three small tone poems: 1890
    Summer Evening
    *Winter Night (Sleigh Ride)
    *Spring Morning
*Paa Vidderne (Sur les cimes)   Symphonic Poem after Henrik Ibsen   1890–2
Over the Hills and Far Away   Fantasy Overture   1895–7
*Appalachia   American Rhapsody   1896
*La Ronde se déroule   Symphonic Poem (also see Life's Dance)   1899
Paris: A Nocturne (The Song of a Great City)   1899

Appendix B—Catalogue of Works

Life's Dance (Lebenstanz) (revised version of *La Ronde se déroule*) 1901; rev. 1912
Brigg Fair: an English Rhapsody 1907
In a Summer Garden Rhapsody 1908; rev. before 1911
A Dance Rhapsody (No. 1) 1908
Summer Night on the River (for small orchestra) 1911
On hearing the first Cuckoo in Spring (for small orchestra) 1912
North Country Sketches: 1913–14
    Autumn (the wind soughs in the trees)
    Winter Landscape
    Dance
    The March of Spring (Woodlands, Meadows and silent Moors)
Air and Dance (for string orchestra) 1915
A Dance Rhapsody No. 2 1916
Eventyr (Once upon a time) Ballad after Asbjørnsen's Folk-lore 1917
A Song before Sunrise (for small orchestra) 1918
*Poem of Life and Love 1918(–19)
A Song of Summer 1929–30
Irmelin Prelude 1931
Fantastic Dance 1931

(b) Solo instrument(s) and orchestra
Suite for violin and orchestra (in four movements, the first entitled
    Pastorale) 1888
Légendes (Sagen) for piano and orchestra (unfinished) 1890
Légende for violin and orchestra (published in version for violin and
    piano) 1895
Piano Concerto in C minor
  *1st version in three movements 1897
  *also as *Fantasy* in one movement
   Further revised and published as *Concerto* in one movement 1906
                    and later
Concerto for violin and cello 1915 (–16)
Concerto for violin 1916
Concerto for cello 1921
Caprice and Elegy for cello and chamber orchestra 1930

(c) Chamber Music
*Romance for violin and piano 1889
*Sonata in B for violin and piano 1892
*Early string quartets 1888, 1893

141

*Romance for cello and piano	1896
Sonata for violin and piano (No. 1)	1905-1914
String Quartet	1916
Sonata for cello and piano	1916
Sonata No. 2 for violin and piano	1924
Sonata No. 3 for violin and piano	1930

(d) Piano solo, etc.

Zum Carnival Polka	1885
*Pensées Mélodieuses	1885
*Badinage	188–?
Two piano pieces: Valse	1889–90
Reverie	
Dance for harpsichord	1919
Five Piano Pieces:	1922–3

        Mazurka and Waltz for a little girl

        Waltz (1891–1922)

        Lullaby for a modern baby (also arr. violin and piano)

        Toccata

Three Preludes	1923

(e) Miscellaneous

In general, arrangements have not been listed but the following titles are added here for clarity:

Norwegian Suite (see *Folkeraadet,* incidental music, above).

Two Aquarelles The *Two songs to be sung of a summer night on the water* arranged for string orchestra by Fenby.

La Calinda Dance from Act II of *Koanga* arranged for orchestra by Fenby.

Late Swallows The third movement of the String Quartet, arranged for string orchestra by Fenby.

The Walk to the Paradise Garden An orchestral interlude between scenes five and six of *A Village Romeo and Juliet.* Other arrangements for conventional orchestra are by Keith Douglas and by Beecham.

APPENDIX C

PERSONALIA

Austin, Frederic (1872–1952), English baritone, composer and arranger. His version of *The Beggar's Opera* was produced at the Lyric Theatre, Hammersmith, in 1920 by Lovat Fraser.

Bantock, Granville (1868–1946), English composer. After studying at the Royal Academy of Music he started the *New Quarterly Musical Review*, toured the world as conductor to a theatrical company, married a poetess (Helen von Schweitzer), became musical director at New Brighton, then Professor of Music at Birmingham University. He wrote many songs, some of which have a distinctly oriental flavour, as well as massive choral works. He was knighted in 1930.

Bartók, Béla (1881–1945), Hungarian composer. Influenced by Brahms and Dohnányi (who was his mentor), also by Liszt, Wagner and Strauss. Together with Kodály he revived the folk tunes of the Magyars.

Beecham, Thomas (1879–1961), son of the proprietor of Beecham's Pills. From 1905 he became known as a conductor, then from 1909 as an impresario in London, particularly of opera. He introduced the Russian Ballet there in 1911, but from 1910 and onwards he concentrated on the propagation of the music of specialized and little-known composers, including Delius. In 1909 he founded the Beecham Symphony Orchestra; in 1932 the London Philharmonic Orchestra; in 1946 the Royal Philharmonic Orchestra. Famous as a wit, raconteur and musical dictator, he was knighted for services to music in 1916, the same year as that in which he succeeded to the family baronetcy. Made C.H. in 1957.

Bjørnson, Bjørnstjerne (1832–1910), Norwegian novelist, poet and dramatist. Diametrically opposed to Ibsen's dicta in that his work breathes happiness, optimism and the joy of living, mainly through adherence to Christian ways. Awarded the Nobel Prize for Literature in 1903.

Busoni, Ferruccio (1886–1924), Italian-German composer, pianist and writer. Composed three operas and a good deal of orchestral and chamber music.

Buths, Julius (1851–1920), German pianist and conductor. Studied in Cologne,

143

Berlin and Paris. Conductor of the Gesangverein of Breslau 1875-9; to Elberfeld 1879-90; then to Düsseldorf 1890-1908, where he was in charge of the Lower Rhine Music Festivals. Translated Elgar's *Dream of Gerontius* into German and was a strong supporter of the music of Delius, especially in Elberfeld.

Cassirer, Fritz (1871-1926), German conductor. Studied in Munich and Berlin, also with Hans Pfitzner. Opera conductor at Lübeck, Posen, Saarbrucken and then Elberfeld (1903-5). Conducted the first performance of *A Village Romeo and Juliet* in Berlin in 1907, and provided the text for Delius's *A Mass of Life*. Later he lived in Munich as a student of philosophy and retired altogether from music.

Chop, Max (1862-1929), German music critic and essayist. After starting life as a law student he turned to music and wrote under the name of 'Monsieur Charles' in Berlin. He wrote early analyses of Liszt's symphonic poems and Wagner's music dramas, and was the first biographer of Delius (1907). He also composed orchestral music, piano pieces and songs, but is chiefly remembered for his penetrating analyses which occupy thirty-six volumes and were written between 1906 and 1924.

Coates, Albert (1882-1953), English-Russian conductor. Born in St Petersburg of a Yorkshire father and Russian mother. Studied conducting under Nikisch, also piano and cello at Leipzig. Conducted in Russia, Germany, England and America. Gave the première of *Song of the High Hills* and the *Requiem* of Delius. Dedicatee of *North Country Sketches*.

Coates, John (1865-1941), English tenor. Began career as baritone with the D'Oyly Carte Company. Début as a tenor came with Stanford's opera *Much Ado about Nothing* in 1901. He remained in opera and was acknowledged as a supreme Wagnerian by 1910. He then sang *Lieder* and oratorio and was outstanding in Elgar's *Dream of Gerontius*.

Cunard, Lady (1872-1948), London hostess and patroness of the arts. Born Maud Alice Burke in New York, she married Sir Bache Cunard in 1895 and left him in 1910. From then on she resided in Cavendish Square, London, and became one the great entertainers and hostesses of society. She had little real knowledge of music but her insatiable appetite for throwing people together and urging them to support her friends made her an invaluable ally to many impresarios and artists between 1910 and 1940.

Dean, Basil (1888-   ), English actor-manager and film director. Assistant producer to Sir Herbert Tree at His Majesty's in 1913, when he secured the rights to produce *Hassan* by James Elroy Flecker. Commissioned Delius to write the incidental music for it. M.B.E., 1918; C.B.E., 1947.

Debussy, Claude Achille (1862–1918), French composer. Friend of Mallarmé and protégé (as was Tchaikovsky) of Mme von Meck. Won the Prix de Rome in 1883. In 1902 composed his only opera, *Pelléas et Mélisande*.

Dent, Edward J. (1876–1957), English musicologist. Important for his researches into early music, for his translations of opera libretti (particularly those of Mozart) into English, and for his definitive biography of Busoni. He was President of the I.S.C.M. between 1923 and 1937; Professor of Music at Cambridge, 1926–41.

Diaghilev, Serge de (1872–1929), Russian impresario of ballet and opera. Brought the Russian Opera (with Chaliapin) to Paris in 1908 and 1909, then to London in 1910. Commissioned leading artists of every kind to work for him, so that his productions reflected the best of modern art. Transformed stage décor and presentation in his lifetime and unintentionally laid the foundations of a permanent ballet in England.

Elgar, Edward (1857–1934), English composer whose determination to succeed overcame all obstacles until he won acceptance at the age of forty-two with his *Variations on an Original Theme* (later to be known as the *Enigma Variations*). Knighted in 1904; baronet in 1931; Master of the King's Musick, 1924–34.

Fenby, Eric (1906–), writer, arranger and composer. Mainly self-taught, was an organist in Scarborough when he wrote to Delius in 1928, offering his services as amanuensis. He succeeded in writing down more than six major compositions at Delius's dictation, and without him it is unlikely that they would ever have been committed to paper. After Delius's death in 1934 he wrote a sensitive description of his time with the composer. He has edited and arranged much of Delius's music. O.B.E., 1962.

Fried, Oskar (1871–1949), German conductor and composer. Originally a horn player, he turned to conducting and became important in Berlin, both with choruses and orchestras. Gave first Berlin performances of *Appalachia* and première of *Life's Dance*. Toured throughout Europe and became conductor of the Tiflis opera in 1934.

Gardiner, Balfour (1877–1950), English composer. Educated at Charterhouse and Oxford. Before 1914 he was active in promoting concerts of young composers' music. He assisted Delius financially by buying the house at Grez, and was a frequent visitor there.

Gauguin, Paul (1848–1903), French painter and sculptor. Was first a sailor, between 1865 and 1871; then a stockbroker; started to paint in that year, 1871. Exhibited his early works and resigned from finance in 1883. Visited Tahiti in 1890. Met Delius in 1891 or 1892 in Paris. Returned to Tahiti and died in the Marquesas in 1903.

Goossens, Eugène (1867–1958), English conductor of Belgian extraction (and with a father and son of the same name). Trained at Brussels Academy and Royal Academy of Music. Conductor of the Carl Rosa Opera, of the Beecham Opera Company in 1917, of *Hassan* at His Majesty's in 1923, and of the British National Opera Company in 1926.

Grainger, Percy (1882–1961), Australian-born composer and pianist. Friend of Grieg and pupil of Busoni. His patient unearthing of individual English folksongs led to the formation of his particularly 'out-of-doors' style of composition. Became a naturalized American. A frequent visitor to Grez and close friend of Delius.

Gregor, Hans (1866–1919), German theatre director. After his appointment in Elberfeld he went to the new Komische Oper in Berlin and thence to the Vienna Opera, where he worked with the great composers and conductors of the post-Mahlerian era of 1911–18, especially with Richard Strauss.

Grieg, Edvard (1843–1907), Norwegian composer. Educated at Leipzig. His Piano Concerto was greatly praised by Liszt. His influence on Grainger and Delius was profound, especially in the importance of folk-music traditions in composition.

Halvorsen, Johan (1864–1935), Norwegian violinist and composer. Studied at Stockholm, Leipzig, Berlin and Liège. Toured as a virtuoso violinist; composed major works reflecting his nationality and his sympathy for Grieg, whose niece he married.

Harrison, Beatrice (1893–1962), English cellist.

Harrison, May (1891–1959), English violinist.

As the 'Harrison sisters' (a third played the piano) they were outstanding executants from an early age. May deputized for Kreisler at the age of eighteen. They were born in India and became students at the Royal College of Music. Together they gave the first performance of Delius's Double Concerto at Queen's Hall in 1920 and were responsible for the choice of Limpsfield, Surrey, as his final place of burial.

Haym, Hans (1860–1921), German conductor. Was diverted by his father from the study of music to philosophy and classical philology in Jena,

Tübingen and Halle. With his doctorate he went to Munich where he studied singing and piano. In 1890 he became music director of the Elber-felder Gesangverein, in succession to Julius Buths (*q.v.*). There he cham-pioned many little-known composers, notably Delius, until Elberfeld became the springboard for Delius's fame in Germany. Haym wrote choral works and songs and was a talented accompanist. In 1912 he bought the plantation at Solano Grove for one of his sons.

Heiberg, Gunnar (1857–1929), Norwegian dramatist. He was influenced by Ibsen's later style. He became director of the Norwegian theatre in Bergen. Published many dramatic criticisms while there, as well as several light, satirical comedies. His *Folkeraadet* was produced in Christiania in 1897 with incidental music by Delius.

Heseltine, Philip (Peter Warlock) (1894–1930), English composer and arranger of Elizabethan lute music. First English biographer of Delius. At first greatly influenced by him, musically and morally, then drew away to others, to return in 1929 as arranger of the London Delius Festival, under Beecham's direction. Died, probably by his own hand, at the early age of thirty-six.

Howard-Jones, Evlyn (1877–1951), English pianist. Trained at the Royal College of Music and privately by Eugen d'Albert. Specialized in Brahms's piano works. Became a successful piano teacher in London where he set up his own school. Excelled in Delius's smaller piano works.

Ibsen, Henrik (1828–1906), Norwegian dramatist, author of twenty-two plays. His *Peer Gynt* had incidental music by Grieg, and it was through Grieg that Delius met him.

Jadassohn, Salomon (1831–1902), German composer and pedagogue. Professor at Leipzig Conservatorium and author of numerous musical text-books. Studied at Breslau and at Weimar under Liszt. Composed in some quantity, including at least three symphonies.

Kodály, Zoltán (1882–1967), Hungarian composer. Studied at the Con-servatoire of Budapest and became a professor there. Together with his friend Bartók (*q.v.*) he collected Hungarian folksongs and used them exten-sively in his own works.

Mucha, Alphonse (1860–1939), Czech artist and one of the founders of the Art Nouveau movement. Arrived in Paris in 1887 and frequented Mère Char-lotte's *crémerie* with Delius and others. He was associated with Sarah

Bernhardt as her scenic and poster designer, and when the cult of Art Nouveau was at its height he went to New York as 'the greatest artist in the world' (1904). Worked with Tiffany, but when the phase was over he left America unnoticed in 1913.

Munch, Edvard (1863–1944), Norwegian painter. He was brought up in Christiania and travelled abroad extensively between 1900 and 1909. His close contact with nature, coupled with periods of mental agitation, produced paintings of gloomy landscapes (sometimes featuring scenes from Ibsen's plays). He exercised a great influence on German expressionism.

Nietzsche, Friedrich (1844–1900), German ethical writer. His works show a strong contempt for the Christian idea of compassion, in opposition to Schopenhauer's asceticism, exaltation of the strong and suppression of the weak. Had an imposing influence and following in Germany at the end of the nineteenth century but died in a lunatic asylum.

O'Neill, Adine (*née* Rückert, d. 1947), English pianist. Descendant of the Belgian family who made harpsichords in the sixteenth and seventeenth centuries. Married to:

O'Neill, Norman (1875–1934), English theatre composer and conductor. He was descended from two former London musical families (Calcott and Horsley). Made a special place for himself as composer of incidental music to plays. One of Delius's closest friends.

Ravel, Maurice (1875–1937), French composer. Studied at Paris Conservatoire under Fauré. His elimination from first place in the Prix de Rome at his fourth attempt resulted in protests and the resignation of the director. His work is often classed with that of Debussy (*q.v.*), since both were Impressionists. His output includes operas, ballets, orchestral music, songs and especially works for the piano.

Reinecke, Carl Heinrich Carsten (1824–1910), German pianist, conductor, composer and arranger. Trained by his father in the violin and started as orchestral player. Came under influence of Mendelssohn and Schumann, and at age of seventeen became court pianist to King Christian VIII of Denmark. After becoming professor of piano at Cologne and undertaking conducting posts in Barmen and Breslau, he was appointed Conductor of the Leipzig Gewandhaus concerts and professor at the Conservatorium there in 1860. While undertaking these posts he composed a great deal and also toured abroad.

Appendix C—Personalia

Sammons, Albert (1886–1957), English violinist. Was heard by Beecham in the restaurant of the Waldorf Hotel in London in 1908 and engaged to lead the Beecham Orchestra. He remained there until 1913. Gave the first performance of Elgar's Violin Concerto and of Delius's Violin Concerto, which he edited.

Schmitt, Florent (1870–1958), French composer. Studied at the Paris Conservatoire under Massenet and Fauré and won the Prix de Rome in 1900. A skilful arranger and orchestrator.

Scott, Charles Kennedy (1876–1965), English choral trainer and reviver of Tudor music. Founded and conducted the Oriana Madrigal Society, which took part in a number of Delius first performances and gave the première of the two unaccompanied choruses *To be sung of a summer night on the water.*

Sinding, Christian (1856–1941), Norwegian composer. First studied in Christiania and was sent on a government scholarship to Leipzig, Dresden, Munich and Berlin. From the age of thirty-four was allowed a pension so that he might compose unimpeded. Friend of Grieg and influenced by him. Taught composition in New York 1921–2, then returned to Norway.

Sitt, Hans (1850–1922), Austro-Bohemian violinist. Studied at the Prague Conservatoire. Was one of the most popular professors at Leipzig, where he also played the viola in the Brodsky Quartet.

Strauss, Richard (1864–1949), German composer, best known for his fifteen operas, some 200 songs and large-scale orchestral works, including seven tone-poems, one inspired by Nietzsche.

Strindberg, August (1849–1912), Swedish dramatist. His best creative period started at the end of the century after an emotional crisis; he had been in the throes of this when Delius met him in Paris. Author of some fifty plays, also poems, novels and stories.

Szántó, Theodor (1877–1934), Hungarian pianist and composer. Studied in Vienna and Budapest and with Busoni in Berlin between 1898 and 1901. Made great use of Japanese themes in his compositions. Edited the solo part of Delius's Piano Concerto which he first gave in 1907 and on tour immediately after.

Tertis, Lionel (1876–), English viola-player. Trained as violinist at Leipzig and the Royal Academy of Music but changed to the far less popular viola, doing more for it than anybody else in this century. Produced the 'Tertis Model' viola and made many arrangements (including some of Delius works) for the instrument.

149

Verlaine, Paul (1844–96), French poet. His works, which are mystical and very musical in construction, appealed greatly to Delius, who knew him in Paris.

Whitehill, Clarence (1871–1940), American operatic baritone. Studied in Chicago and Paris, and was the first male American singer to appear at the Opéra-Comique. Sang at Bayreuth in 1904 and again in 1908 and 1909. A celebrated Wagnerian interpreter. The first Koanga at Elberfeld in 1904.

Warlock, Peter. See *Heseltine, Philip.*

Wood, Henry J. (1869–1944), English conductor. Organist at the age of ten; studied at the Royal Academy of Music; conducted his first opera when he was nineteen and at twenty-five was engaged as conductor of the Queen's Hall Promenade Concerts (1895). There he remained to educate the London musical public and to train generations of players until his last illness. Knighted in 1911.

APPENDIX D

BIBLIOGRAPHY

(This bibliography has been specially prepared for the present work by Lionel Carley, Archivist to the Delius Trust.)

Abraham, Gerald, 'Delius and his Literary Sources'. (*Music and Letters,* London, April 1929; reprinted in his 'Slavonic and Romantic Music', Faber, London, 1968.)

Ackere, Jules Van, 'Un musicien méconnu: Frederick Delius, coloriste'. (*Revue générale belge,* Brussels, May 1968.)

Armstrong, Thomas, 'Delius Today' (in 'Delius': programme brochure for the Delius Centenary Festival, Bradford, 1962).

Backhouse, J. M., 'Delius Letters'. (*British Museum Quarterly,* London, Autumn 1965.)

Barjansky, Catherine, 'Portraits with Backgrounds'. (Macmillan, New York, 1947; Geoffrey Bles, London, 1948.)

Baum, Marie-Luise, 'Hans Haym' (in 'Beiträge zur Geschichte und Heimatkunde des Wuppertals, 17, Wuppertaler Biographien, 9'; Born-Verlag, Wuppertal, 1970).

Beecham, Thomas, 'Frederick Delius'. (Hutchinson, London, 1959; Knopf, New York, 1960.)

—— 'A Mingled Chime: An Autobiography'. (G. P. Putnam's Sons, New York, 1943.) Reprinted as 'A Mingled Chime: Leaves from an Autobiography'. (Hutchinson, London, 1944.)

Blom, Eric, 'Delius and America'. (*The Musical Quarterly,* New York, July 1929.)

—— 'Stepchildren of Music'. (Foulis, London, n.d.)

Brian, Havergal, 'The Art of Delius'. (*Musical Opinion,* London, March–October 1924.)

Cardus, Neville, 'Ten Composers'. (Cape, London, 1945.) Revised as 'A Composer's Eleven'. (Cape, London, 1958.)

Carley, Lionel, 'Jelka Rosen Delius: Artist, Admirer and Friend of Rodin. The Correspondence 1900–1914'. (*Nottingham French Studies*, Nottingham, May and October 1970.)

Chop, Max, 'Frederick Delius'. (Harmonie, Berlin, 1907.)

—— 'Frederick Delius' (in 'Monographien Moderner Musiker', Vol. II; C. F. Kahnt Nachfolger, Leipzig, 1907).

Cooke, Deryck, 'Delius & Form: A Vindication'. (*The Musical Times*, London, June–July 1962.)

—— 'The Delius Centenary: A Summing-up'. (*Musical Opinion*, London, June–August 1962.)

—— 'Delius's Operatic Masterpiece'. (*Opera*, London, April 1962. See also June 1962.)

—— 'Delius the Unknown'. (*Proceedings of the Royal Musical Association*, London, 1962–3.)

—— 'Delius: A Centenary Evaluation' (in 'Essays on Music: an anthology from *The Listener*', ed. F. Aprahamian, Cassell, London, 1967).

Copley, I. A., 'Warlock and Delius—A Catalogue'. (*Music and Letters*, London, July 1968.)

Delius, Clare, 'Frederick Delius: Memories of My Brother'. (Ivor Nicholson and Watson, London, 1935.)

Delius, Frederick, 'At the Cross-Roads'. (*The Sackbut*, London, September 1920.) Reprinted as 'The Present Cult: Charlatanism and Humbug in Music'. (*The British Musician and Musical News*, Birmingham, November 1929.) See also 'Composers on Music: An Anthology of Composers' Writings', ed. S. Morgenstern (Faber, London, 1958).

—— 'The Future of Opera' (newspaper interview [1919] reprinted in 'Composers on Music').

—— 'Musik in England im Kriege'. (*Musikblätter des Anbruch*, Vienna, November 1919.)

—— 'Recollections of Strindberg'. (*The Sackbut*, London, December 1920.) Reprinted in *Heseltine*: 'Frederick Delius', *q.v.*

—— and Papus, 'Anatomie et Physiologie de l'Orchestre'. (Chamuel, Paris, 1894.)

Delius Society Newsletter (quarterly, published by the Delius Society of Great Britain, London, 1963–   ).

Demuth, Norman, 'Musical Trends in the 20th Century'. (Rockliff, London, 1952.)

Dieren, Bernard van, 'Frederick Delius'. (*The Musical Times*, London, July

1934.) Reprinted in part in 'The Book of Modern Composers', ed. David Ewen (Knopf, New York, 1942).

Elgar, Edward, 'My Visit to Delius' (newspaper article [1933] reprinted in *The British Musician and Musical News,* Birmingham, May 1934; and in *Choir,* London, July 1934).
Exhibition catalogue: 'Delius Centenary Festival: Frederick Delius 1862–1934'. (Bradford City Art Gallery and Museums, March 30–May 13 1962.)
—— 'Frederick Delius: Centenary Festival Exhibition'. (The Royal Festival Hall, London, June 1–June 21 1962.) An amended version of the original catalogue issued at Bradford.

Fenby, Eric, 'Delius'. ('The Great Composers' series, Faber, London, 1971.)
—— 'Delius as I knew him'. (Bell, London, 1936; reprinted Quality Press, London, 1948; revised and edited by the author, with an Introduction by Sir Malcolm Sargent, Icon Books, London, 1966.)
—— 'A Village Romeo and Juliet: Foreword and Analysis of the Records'. (Issued for The Delius Fellowship by The Gramophone Company Ltd, Hayes, Middlesex, 1948.)
Findon, B. W. (ed.), 'Hassan'. (*The Play Pictorial,* London, Vol. 43, No. 261, n.d.) A description of the 1923 production, with many photographs.
Foss, Hubert, 'The Instrumental Music of Frederick Delius'. (*Tempo,* 'Delius Number', London, Winter 1952–3.)
—— See *Heseltine:* 'Frederick Delius'. (Revised edition.)

Grainger, Percy Aldridge, 'About Delius' (in *Heseltine:* 'Frederick Delius', revised edition, *q.v.*).
—— 'Impressions of Art in Europe. Article 3—Delius Reaps His Harvest'. (*Musical Courier,* New York, 28 September 1929.)
—— 'The Personality of Frederick Delius'. (*The Australian Musical News,* Melbourne, 1 July 1934.)
Gray, Cecil, 'Musical Chairs: An Autobiography'. (Home & Van Thal, London, 1948.)
—— 'Peter Warlock: A Memoir of Philip Heseltine'. (Cape, London, 1934.)
—— 'A Survey of Contemporary Music'. (O.U.P., London, 1924.)
Grew, Sydney, 'Our Favourite Musicians'. (Foulis, Edinburgh and London, 1922.)
Grier, Christopher, 'Frederick Delius' (in 'The Music Masters', Vol. 3, ed. A. L. Bacharach, Cassell, London, 1952; reprinted Pelican Books, London, 1958).

Haddon-Squire, W. H., 'Delius and Warlock'. (*Tempo,* 'Delius Number', Winter 1952–3.)

Hanson, Lawrence & Elisabeth, 'The Noble Savage: A Life of Paul Gauguin'. (Chatto & Windus, London, 1954; reprinted Arrow Books, London, 1960.)

Harrison, May, 'The Music of Delius'. (*Proceedings of the Royal Musical Association,* London, 1944–5.)

Haym, Hans, 'Delius: A Mass of Life. Introduction to the Words and Music'. (Universal-Edition, No. 8256, Vienna–New York, 1925.)

Heseltine, Philip (Peter Warlock), 'Delius's New Opera'. (*The Musical Times,* London, April 1920.)

—— 'Frederick Delius'. (John Lane, The Bodley Head, London, 1923.) Reprinted with additions, annotations and comments, by Hubert Foss (The Bodley Head, London, 1952).

—— 'Introductions, V: Frederick Delius'. (*The Music Bulletin,* London, May 1923.)

—— 'Some Notes on Delius and His Music'. (*The Musical Times,* London, March 1915.)

Hill, Ralph, 'Frederick Delius' (in 'British Music of our Time', ed. A. L. Bacharach, Pelican Books, London, 1946).

Hogarth, Basil, 'Frederick Delius: A Critical Estimate'. (*The English Review,* London, August 1934.)

Holbrooke, Joseph, 'Contemporary British Composers'. (Cecil Palmer, London, 1925.)

Holland, A. K., 'Delius as a Song Writer'. (*Tempo,* 'Delius Number', London, Winter 1952–3.)

—— Notes for *The Delius Society* record albums: 1934, 1936 and 1938.

—— 'The Songs of Delius'. (*Musical Opinion,* Vol. 60, London, 1936; collected and reprinted under the same title in 'The Musical Pilgrim' series, O.U.P., London, 1951.)

Howes, Frank, 'The English Musical Renaissance'. (Secker & Warburg, London, 1966.)

Hudson, Derek, 'Norman O'Neill: A Life of Music'. (Quality Press, London, 1945.)

Hull, Robert H., 'Delius'. (Hogarth, London, 1928.)

—— 'The Music of Frederick Delius'. (*Contemporary Review,* London, October 1929.)

Hull, Robin, 'The Scope of Delius'. (*The Music Review,* Cambridge, November 1942.)

Appendix D—Bibliography

Hutchings, Arthur, 'The Chamber Works of Delius'. (*The Musical Times*, London, January, March, April and May 1935.)
—— 'Delius'. (Macmillan, London, 1948.)
—— 'Delius's Operas'. (*Tempo*, 'Delius Number', London, Winter 1952–3.)
—— 'Frederick Delius' (in 'The Concerto', ed. Ralph Hill, Pelican Books, London, 1952).

Jahoda, Gloria, 'The Road to Samarkand: Frederick Delius and His Music'. (Scribner's, New York, 1969.)

Klein, John W., 'Delius as a Musical Dramatist'. (*The Music Review*, Cambridge, November 1961.)
—— 'Delius's Advance to Mastery'. (*Tempo*, London, Winter 1961–2.)

Lowe, Rachel, 'Delius's First Performance'. (*The Musical Times*, London, March 1965.)
—— 'The Delius Trust Manuscripts'. (*Brio*, London, Spring and Autumn 1968.)
Lyle, Robert, 'Delius and the Philosophy of Romanticism'. (*Music and Letters*, London, April 1948.)

Marx, Joseph, 'Frederick Delius'. (*Musikblätter des Anbruch*, Vienna, November 1919.)
Mellers, W. H., 'Peter Warlock'. (*Scrutiny*, Cambridge, March 1937.)
Mitchell, Donald, 'Delius: The Choral Music'. (*Tempo*, 'Delius Number', London, Winter 1952–3.)
Mucha, Jiří, 'Alphonse Mucha: His Life and Art'. (Heinemann, London, 1966.)

Nettel, R., 'Music in the Five Towns 1840–1914'. (O.U.P., London, 1944.)

Orr, C. W., 'Frederick Delius: Some Personal Recollections'. (*Musical Opinion*, London, August 1934.)
Oyler, Philip, 'Sons of the Generous Earth'. (Hodder & Stoughton, London, 1963.)

Palmer, Christopher, 'Delius and Poetic Realism'. (*Music and Letters*, London, October 1970).
—— 'Delius, Vaughan Williams and Debussy'. (*Music and Letters*, London, October 1969.)

Payne, Anthony, 'Delius's Requiem'. (*Tempo,* London, Spring 1966.)
—— 'Delius's Stylistic Development'. (*Tempo,* London, Winter 1961–2.)
Perruchot, Henri, 'Gauguin'. Translated from the French by Humphrey Hare. (Perpetua Books, London, 1963.)
Pirie, Peter J., 'Delius the Unknown'. (*Music and Musicians,* London, July 1971.)
—— 'Epitaph on a Centenary'. (*The Music Review,* Cambridge, August 1962.)

Randel, William, '"Koanga" and its Libretto'. (*Music and Letters,* London, April 1971.)
Redwood, Christopher, 'Fennimore and Gerda'. (*Composer,* London, Spring 1968.)
Reid, Charles, 'Britain from Stanford to Vaughan Williams' (in 'Choral Music', ed. Arthur Jacobs, Pelican Books, London, 1963).
—— 'Thomas Beecham: An Independent Biography'. (Gollancz, London, 1961.)

Sadler, Fernande, 'Grès-sur-Loing: Notice historique'. (M. Bourges, Fontaine-bleau, 1906.)
—— 'L'Hôtel Chevillon et les artistes de Grès-sur-Loing'. (L'Informateur de Seine-et-Marne, Fontainebleau, n.d.)
Scott, Charles Kennedy, Notes on Delius, followed by seven letters from Delius to the author (in *Heseltine*: 'Frederick Delius', Revised edition, *q.v.*).
Simon, Heinrich, 'Frederick Delius'. Translated by H. Grunbaum. (*Musical Opinion,* London, February–March 1935.)
—— 'Frederick Delius: Zum 60. Geburtstag'. (*Musikblätter des Anbruch,* Vienna, January–February 1923.)
Smith, John Boulton, 'Portrait of a Friendship: Edvard Munch and Frederick Delius'. (*Apollo,* London, January 1966.)
Smyth, Ethel, 'Beecham and Pharaoh'. (Chapman & Hall, London, 1935.)
Stevenson, Robert Louis, 'Essays of Travel'. (Chatto & Windus, London, 1905.)
Stewart, Reid, 'The String Music of Delius'. (*The Strad,* London, May, September and October 1935, and June 1936.)
Streatfeild, Richard Alexander, 'Musiciens Anglais Contemporains'. Traduction française de Louis Pennequin. (Éditions du Temps Présent, Paris, 1913.)

Threlfall, Robert, 'Delius in Eric Fenby's MSS.'. (*Composer,* London, Spring 1969.)
—— 'Delius's Second Thoughts, and an Unknown Version of His Piano Concerto'. (*Musical Opinion,* London, August 1970.)

Appendix D—Bibliography

Tucker, Norman, 'A Village Romeo and Juliet' (in 'Delius': programme brochure for the Delius Centenary Festival, Bradford, 1962).

Upton, Stuart, and Walker, Malcolm, 'Frederick Delius: A Discography'. (Delius Society of Great Britain, London, 1969.)

Warlock, Peter, see Heseltine, Philip.
Wood, Henry J., 'My Life of Music'. (Gollancz, London, 1938.)

Young, Percy M., 'A History of British Music'. (Benn, London, 1967.)

APPENDIX E

IT WAS not chance that took Jelka Rosen, and thus Delius, to Grez. They might have found another quiet place in which to live and to work, but that would not have been the same thing at all. Grez is a magical place, as any visitor today will confirm.

At one time Grès, a seigneurie of the Duchy of Nemours, was an important town whose inhabitants were wine-growers and foresters. Its recorded history goes back to 1067, the year after the Norman Conquest of Britain, when the Grézieaux (as the inhabitants are called) sought protection from the new Duke of Normandy, Robert le Diable, against local, upstart, predatory dukes. After the seventeenth century, when radical changes in temperature and weather, coupled with local banditry, destroyed the vineyards for ever, Grez settled down on the edge of the Fontainebleau forest to mind its own business and to eschew politics for ever.

It was near Grez, in the forest, where the remaining ensigns of Napoleon's vanquished army burned their standards after Waterloo and drank the ashes in brandy to avoid their capture. But history is evident in Grez even today. The ruined Donjon, which goes back to the twelfth century, still harbours jackdaws (descendants of 'Koanga' perhaps) and has looked out on many battles and scenes of desolation. The last one there was in 1944 when the historic bridge across the River Loing was blown up: some say by the retreating Wehrmacht, others say by the Maquis. But fortunately only the two centre spans were destroyed and the rest remains.

Grez had two periods of glory, from the time when it ceased to have any political influence or importance. The first of these was in 1830 when Corot settled in Barbizon (to the north-west of Fontainebleau town) and established his school of 'nature painters'. This resulted in the so-called Barbizon School being founded to extend Corot's ideals, and between 1850 and 1860 Rousseau led a fervent team of painters to see the beauty existing in trees, in sunlight on leaves, and in God's own objects. Among the artists who accompanied him were Millet, Daubigny, Diaz and Courbet, all belonging to the Paris of Puccini's *La Bohème*. When they were not utterly absorbed in their work they were as wild and as gay as one can imagine. They were, for the most part, impecunious, and travelled about on foot, landing up for the night wherever they found sympathetic treatment, opportunities for their practical jokes and subjects for painting. One of the places which took their activities in good part was Grez-sur-Loing, which they visited; they drank at the village's only hotel, the Chevillon (still existing, but not as an hotel). Robert Louis Stevenson visited them there in 1875–6, during the after-math of the Siege of Paris, and has given a vivid account in his book [1] under the chapter called 'Forest Notes'. He also tells of the Mère Antoine and her famous inn at Marlotte, close to Grez (where in Delius's time 'Joe' Heseltine lived, carrying on the painting tradition with something less than the dexterity of the former masters). A scene from the inn as it was at the time of the Impressionist painters has been perpetuated by Renoir's picture showing Sisley, Frank Lamy, Pissarro and the three-legged dog Toto.

Stevenson found Grez extremely attractive, stayed at the Chevillon and fell in love with his future wife there. By the end of the nineteenth century, when the artistic revels at the Chevillon had somewhat quietened down, people came there for sentimental reasons and simply to paint; Jelka Rosen happened to be one of them. She and her mother often stayed there while Jelka was painting in the Marquis's garden. Opposite page 100 is a picture which shows a group of artists of the Barbizon School, in the 1870s. In it are Stevenson, an American artist called Chadwick, Corot, and an Irishman, Frank O'Meara. Chadwick married another visitor to Grez, the Swedish painter and engraver Emma Löwstädt. Between 1884 and 1894 they rented from the Marquis de Carzeaux the house which was later to be associated with Delius; their daughter Madame Louise Courmes lived in Grez until her death in February 1971. She possessed a painting by her father of her mother and herself in the garden.

Next an American artist called Lee Robbins took the house and left it

---

[1] *Essays of Travel* (London, 1905).

to marry the Dutch painter Van Rinkhuyzen. It was empty for a short while until it was sold by the Marquis to Jelka Rosen and her mother. In the 1920s Balfour Gardiner offered to help the Deliuses financially by taking full responsibility for the house so that they would pay him only a peppercorn rent. The property would revert to him on Jelka's death, as the most probable course of events was thought to be that Delius would die first. As Delius and Jelka had no children this arrangement helped them a good deal.

In 1935, when Jelka died, the house remained empty for nearly a year. Many of Delius's papers were burned, others were removed by Beecham, Fenby, Delius's sister Clare and her daughter Margaret. The house was then bought from Balfour Gardiner in 1937 by Professor Merle d'Aubigné, the celebrated orthopaedic surgeon, and Madame d'Aubigné. They altered it very little as far as the exterior of the house shows. The most radical change is in the conversion of Delius's music room into several bedrooms, the removal of the staircase which led up to it and the amalgamation of the small wing which housed Fenby's room, now all part of the bedroom arrangement on the first floor. The original two houses are very much one today, and have undergone modernization by a complete central heating system. On the other hand, Jelka's studio is almost exactly as she left it, even to her daubs of paint on the inside of one of the doors, that served as a pallette.

When one looks at the house from the main village street in which it stands, it is both imposing and a little forbidding. The dark green shutters and the huge, dark green gateway (through which a bus might pass) have a closed feeling inside the white plaster walls. The front wall is as a barricade between the street, which is the world, and the house and garden beyond. This is understandable when one goes through, because inside it is a kind of little paradise. At the opposite end of the garden flows the Loing, Styx-like, as a barrier there, and the view is for ever preserved because a plot of land on the opposite meadow has been bought and is included in the estate. The French fondness for *le camping* is too formidable an occupation to be ignored.

Stevenson tells us that when he asked about Grez outside it he always got the reply 'Il y a de l'eau!' (There's water there!) And as Grez is only 64 km. from Paris, with the Route Nationale 7 and a new motorway passing close by, it is an ideal retreat for the weekend. Any property that now comes up for sale is snapped up by Parisians and so the village is slowly being peopled by strangers. The Grézieaux resent this but there is nothing that they can do to prevent it.

I said earlier that Grez had two periods of glory and that the first of these was caused by the influx of the Barbizon painters and their disciples. The second, I have no hesitation in saying, was between 1897 and 1935 when Jelka and Frederick Delius lived there. They did not much enter into village life, it is true, but they contributed to making Grez a focal point for many artists and musicians who came to Paris or farther south. Neither Yorkshire, nor Florida, nor even the village of Limpsfield which now nurses his bones were his home. Grez was his home and the music of Delius is something of which Grez can fairly claim a full share.

APPENDIX F

GAUGUIN'S 'NEVERMORE'

IT SHOWS something of Delius's artistic perception that he should have bought a Gauguin painting as early as 1898 when few people realized the integrity and genius of the tortured Breton artist. Gauguin wrote to his artist friend and agent Georges-Daniel de Monfreid on 14th February 1897 from Tahiti, telling him about the new picture, called *Never-more*, which he had finished. Delius paid de Monfreid 500 francs on 11th November 1898, and de Monfreid despatched this sum to Gauguin on the same day. Delius received the picture in Paris. The artist's description is this:

I wanted to suggest by means of a simple nude a certain long-lost barbarian luxury. The whole is drowned in colours which are deliberately sombre and sad; it is neither silk, nor velvet, nor batiste, nor gold that creates luxury here but simply matter which has been enriched by the hand of artist. No non-sense . . . man's imagination alone has enriched the dwelling with his fantasy. As a title *Nevermore*: not the raven of Edgar [Allan] Poe, but the bird of the devil that is keeping watch. It is badly painted (I'm so nervy and can only work in bouts) but no matter, I think it is a good canvas.

The importance which Gauguin attached to this painting is evident by his request to de Monfreid to include it in a retrospective exhibition of his works. A few years later de Monfreid borrowed the canvas from Delius for such an occasion and then had it carefully restored on Delius's behalf. When he heard who had bought the painting, Gauguin wrote to de Monfreid on 12th January 1899 saying:

I am very happy that Delius is the owner [of the painting], since it is not a speculative purchase with the intention of resale but one made because he admires it.

The tone of this letter and that of the earlier one shows an unshakeable faith in his own work and an absolute certainty that one day his pictures

162

would possess immense value. In this respect Delius was equally confident in his own achievements and lived to see them bear fruit—which Gauguin never did.

It was only a severe financial crisis which made it necessary for Delius to part with *Nevermore* in 1923. Yet he was not without it completely for Jelka had made a good copy of the canvas. The original was bought by Alexander Reid of Glasgow who passed it on very quickly to Messrs Agnew. They exhibited it in their Manchester show-room in September 1923 where it was shown as No. 17 in an Exhibition of Masterpieces of French Art. Agnews then sold *Nevermore* to Herbert Coleman of Manchester and he in turn disposed of it to Samuel Courtauld, probably in July 1924. It appeared in a Gauguin Exhibition at the Leicester Square Galleries, London, where it was No. 52, and was also reproduced in the catalogue. It is now in the Courtauld Institute Galleries in Woburn Square, London. It measures $23\frac{3}{8}$ in. by $45\frac{5}{8}$ in. (84·8 cm. by 115·8 cm.).[1]

---

[1] I am most grateful to the Curator of the Collections of the Courtauld Institute and to Dr Lionel Carley, Archivist to the Delius Trust, for having supplied me with the bulk of the above information.

APPENDIX G

Artistic Director and Conductor-in-Chief: Sir Thomas Beecham, Bart.

(1) 12th October at Queen's Hall (Orchestra of the Columbian Gramophone Co.)

Brigg Fair (1907)
A Late Lark (First performance) (1925)
Dance Rhapsody No. 2 (1916)
Sea-Drift (Dennis Noble; London Select Choir) (1903)
In a Summer Garden (1908)
A Village Romeo and Juliet (excerpt sung by Pauline Maunder, Heddle Nash
and London Select Choir) (1900–1)

(2) 16th October at Aeolian Hall (Orchestra led by Charles Woodhouse)

A Song before Sunrise (1918)
Seven Songs for voice and piano (Olga Haley acc. by Evlyn Howard-
Jones)
 Heimkehr (1889)
 Verborg'ne Liebe (1890)
 Beim Sonnenuntergang (1888)
 Sehnsucht (1888)
 Le ciel est pardessus le toit (1895)
 In the Seraglio Garden (1897)
 Eine Vogelweise (1889)
Sonata for Cello and Piano (1916) (Beatrice Harrison and Evlyn Howard-
Jones)
Summer Night on the River (1911)
Air and Dance (First Performance) (1915)
Six Songs for voice and piano (John Goss acc. by Evlyn Howard-Jones)
 Black Roses (1901)
 Chanson d'automne (1911)
 Silken Shoes (1897)

    I-Brasil (1913)
    Das Veilchen (1900)
    Spielmann (1890)
Nine Piano Pieces (Evlyn Howard-Jones)
    Three Preludes (1923)
    Dance (originally for harpsichord—1919)
    Five Pieces (1923)
Six Songs for voice and piano (John Armstrong acc. by Evlyn Howard-Jones)
    Irmelin [*Rose*] (1897)
    To Daffodils (1915)
    The Nightingale has a Lyre of Gold (1910)
    Il pleure dans mon cœur (1895)
    So white, so soft, so sweet is she (1915)
    Let Springtime come then (1897)
On Hearing the First Cuckoo in Spring (1912)

(3) 18th October at Queen's Hall (B.B.C. Orchestra, Leader Arthur Catterall)
    Eventyr (1917)
    Cynara (First performance) (1907) (John Goss)
    Concerto for Piano and Orchestra (Revised 1906) (Evlyn Howard-Jones)
    Arabesk (1911) (John Goss, London Select Choir)
    Appalachia (1902) (Royal College Choral Class and B.B.C. National Chorus)

(4) 23rd October at Aeolian Hall
    Three unaccompanied Choruses (London Select Choir)
        The Splendour Falls (1923)
        On Craig Ddu (1907)
        Midsummer Song (1908)
    Four Songs for voice and piano: (Dora Labbette acc. by Evlyn Howard-Jones)
        The Nightingale (1888)
        Autumn (1900)
        La Lune blanche (1910)
        Klein Venevil (1889–90)
    Sonata No. 1 for violin and piano (1905–14). Arthur Catterall and Evlyn Howard-Jones

Three Songs for voice and piano (Heddle Nash acc. by Evlyn Howard-Jones)

    Indian Love-song (1891)

    Love's Philosophy (1891)

    To the Queen of my Heart (1891)

Two unaccompanied Choruses (*To be sung of a summer night on the water*) (London Select Choir)

Four Songs for voice and piano (Dora Labbette acc. by Evlyn Howard-Jones)

    Twilight Fancies (1889)

    Am schönsten Sommerabend war's (1888)

    Margaret's Lullaby (1889)

    Spring, the sweet Spring (1915)

String Quartet (1916) (Virtuoso String Quartet: Marjorie Hayward, Edwin Virgo, Raymond Jeremy, Cedric Sharpe)

(5) 24th October at Queen's Hall (Royal Philharmonic Orchestra)

    North Country Sketches (1913–14)

    Songs of Sunset (1906–7) (Olga Haley, John Goss, London Select Choir)

    Violin Concerto (1916) (Albert Sammons)

    Dance Rhapsody No. 1 (1908)

    Gerda (First performance in England) (1910) (Pauline Maunder, John Goss, London Select Choir)

(6) 1st November at Queen's Hall (B.B.C. Orchestra, Leader Charles Wood-house, Philharmonic Choir: Charles Kennedy Scott)

    A Mass of Life (1904–5). Miriam Licette (sop.); Astra Desmond (contralto); Tudor Davies (tenor); Roy Henderson (baritone)

DELIUS FESTIVAL: OCTOBER TO DECEMBER 1946
(SEVEN CONCERTS)

Artistic Director and Conductor-in-Chief: Sir Thomas Beecham, Bart. With the Royal Philharmonic Orchestra (except 11th December)

(1) 26th October at Royal Albert Hall (London début of R.P.O.)

    Over the Hills and Far Away (1895–7)

    The Song of the High Hills (Freda Hart and Leslie Jones) (1911)

Appendix G—Delius Festivals

Incidental Music to *Hassan* (1920-3)
Appalachia (Bruce Clark) (1902)
  With the Luton Choral Society

(2) 4th November at Royal Albert Hall
Paris: the Song of a Great City (1899)
Piano Concerto (Betty Humby-Beecham) (1906)
Sea-Drift (Redvers Llewellyn) (1903)
On Hearing the First Cuckoo in Spring (1912)
First *Dance Rhapsody* (1908)
  With the B.B.C. Choral Society

(3) 8th November at Royal Albert Hall
Sur les Cimes ('first performance') (1890-2)
In a Summer Garden (1908)
Concerto for Violin and Orchestra (Jean Pougnet) (1916)
Koanga: Act III (conducted by Richard Austin) (1895-7)
  (Victoria Sladen, Leslie Jones, Roderick Jones, Trevor Anthony, Bruce
  Clark and the Croydon Philharmonic Society)

(4) 15th November at Royal Albert Hall
Eventyr: Once upon a time (1917)
Brigg Fair: An English Rhapsody (1901)
Songs of Sunset (1906-7)
  (Nancy Evans, Redvers Llewellyn and the B.B.C. Choral Society)
A Village Romeo and Juliet: Act III (conducted by Richard Austin
  (1900-1)
  (Freda Hart, Estelle Applin, Ethel Lyon, Eileen Pilcher, Heddle Nash,
  Leslie Jones, George Prangnell, Bruce Clark, Redvers Llewellyn and the
  B.B.C. Choral Society)

(5) 18th November at Central Hall, Westminster
Second Dance Rhapsody (1916)
Idyll for soprano, baritone and orchestra (1932). (Elsie Suddaby and
  Roderick Jones)
Songs of Farewell (Croydon Philharmonic Society) (1930)

167

Three small tone poems (1890):
    Summer Evening
    Winter Night
    Spring Morning
Songs with orchestra (Elsie Suddaby):
    The Violet ⎫
    Twilight Fancies ⎬ (orch. Beecham)
    Autumn ⎭
    Il pleure dans mon cœur ⎫
    The Bird's Story   ⎬ (orch. Delius)
Summer Night on the River (1911)
A Song before Sunrise (1918)
Cynara (Roderick Jones) (1907)
Concerto for Violin, Cello and Orchestra (Paul Beard and Anthony Pini) (1915)

(6) 21st November at Central Hall, Westminster
North Country Sketches (1913–14)
Three part-songs: *The Splendour Falls*
                 On Craig Ddu
                 Midsummer Song
Arabesk [1] (Gordon Clinton; conducted by Richard Austin) (1911)
Songs with orchestra (Marjorie Thomas):
    In the Seraglio garden (orch. Delius)
    Black Roses (orch. Del Mar)
    I-Brasil (orch. Delius)
    Le ciel est pardessus le toit (orch. Delius)
    The homeward journey (orch. Sondheimer)
Irmelin Prelude (1931)
Marche Caprice (1888)
Songs with orchetra (John Kentish):
    A Late Lark (orch. Delius)
    The Nightingale has a lyre of gold (orch. Del Mar)
    Irmelin [Rose] ⎫
    La Lune blanche ⎬ (orch. Delius)
    To Daffodils (orch. Del Mar)
La Calinda (arr. Fenby, 1938)

---

[1] Spelt *Arabesque* in the programme.

Appendix G—Delius Festivals

Folkeraadet: Prelude to Act III (1897)
  With the Luton Choral Society

(7) 11th December at Royal Albert Hall
  A Mass of Life (1904–5). Stiles-Allen (soprano); Muriel Brunskill (contralto); Francis Russell (tenor); Redvers Llewellyn (baritone); with the
  B.B.C. Symphony Orchestra and the B.B.C. Choral Society conducted
  by Sir Thomas Beecham, Bart.

DELIUS CENTENARY FESTIVAL AT BRADFORD, YORKS,
MARCH TO APRIL 1962 (FOUR CONCERTS AND OPERA)

(1) 29th March Gala Performance in St George's Hall
  A Dance Rhapsody (No. 1) (1908)
  Sea-Drift (Thomas Hemsley) (1903)
  In a Summer Garden (1908)
  The Song of the High Hills (1911)
    With the Bradford Old Choral Society and the Royal Philharmonic
    Orchestra conducted by Rudolf Kempe

(2) 30th March in St George's Hall
  Paris: The Song of a Great City (1899)
  Concerto for Violin and Orchestra (Raymond Cohen) (1916)
  Brigg Fair: An English Rhapsody (1907)
  North Country Sketches (1913–14)
    With the Royal Philharmonic Orchestra conducted by Rudolf Kempe

(3) 31st March in St George's Hall
  Songs of Farewell (1930)
  Appalachia (1902)
  Eventyr: Once upon a Time (1917)
  Songs of Sunset (1906–7) (Marjorie Thomas and Thomas Stewart)
    With the Bradford Festival Choral Society and the Royal Philharmonic
    Orchestra conducted by Rudolf Kempe

(4) 2nd April at Bradford Grammar School

Sonata No. 1 for Violin and Piano (1905–14) (Raymond Cohen and Gerald Moore)

Songs (Gerald English, tenor):
  La Lune blanche (1910)
  Il pleure dans mon cœur (1895)
  Le ciel est pardessus le toit (1895)
  Chanson d'Automne (1911)
  Avant que tu ne t'en ailles (1919)

Sonata No. 2 for Violin and Piano (1924). (Raymond Cohen and Gerald Moore)

Songs (Marjorie Thomas, contralto):
  It was a lover and his lass (1916)
  So white, so soft, so sweet (1915)
  I-Brasil (1913)
  Spring, the sweet Spring (1915)
  To Daffodils (1915)

String Quartet (1916) (The Allegri String Quartet)

(5) 3rd, 5th, 7th April at Alhambra Theatre: The Sadler's Wells Opera
  A Village Romeo and Juliet

MANZ	Lawrence Folley
MARTI	Donald McIntyre
SALI, AS A CHILD	Soo Bee Lee
VRENCHEN, AS A CHILD	Sheila Amit
SALI, AS A YOUNG MAN	John Wakefield
VRENCHEN, AS A YOUNG GIRL	Elsie Morison
THE DARK FIDDLER	Neil Easton

Sadler's Wells Orchestra conducted by Meredith Davies
Producer: Basil Coleman   *Designer:* Leslie Hurry

INDEX

Compositions by Delius are shown alphabetically in the index. Compositions by other composers are shown under those composers' names. Bold figures refer to pages on which compositions are analysed in detail.

Index

Index

Index

Index